A QUAKER'S VIEW OF GENDLIN'S PHILOSOPHY

CROSSING EUGENE GENDLIN'S IMPLICIT AND THE QUAKER'S LIGHT WITHIN

HARBERT RICE

EMBUDO VALLEY PRESS

A QUAKER'S VIEW OF GENDLIN'S PHILSOPHY
CROSSING EUGENE GENDLIN'S IMPLICIT AND THE QUAKER'S LIGHT WITHIN
BY HARBERT RICE

Embudo Valley Press
P.O. Box 538
Dixon, NM 87527

embudovalleypress@gmail.com
www.embudovalleypress.com

Copyright © 2020 by Harbert Rice
All rights reserved.

ISBN (Print book): 978-1-7346533-0-4

ISBN (E-Book): 978-1-7346533-1-1

Library of Congress Control Number: 2020934078

First Edition. Printed in the United States of America

Cover and Interior Design by One On One Book Production and Marketing, West Hills, California

Please address reproduction requests to:

>Harbert Rice
>Embudo Valley Press
>embudovalleypress@gmail.com

ACKNOWLEGMENTS

My thanks to all those who contributed to this book by commenting on various drafts as the book evolved.

My special thanks to Rob Foxcroft and Helen Meads who provided insights into both early and contemporary Quaker history, and helped me get my Quaker details right.

My special thanks also to Neli Dunaetz who vetted my use of and interpretation of Gendlin's A Process Model. Neil helped me avoid swamping the reader with an introductory stream of Gendlin's philosophical concepts. He helped me add Gendlin's concepts as the needs arose in the course of the text.

Harbert Rice

CONTENTS

Acknowledgments	iii
1. Introduction	1
2. Getting Started	5
3. Quaker Practice	9
4. An Underlying Social Process	35
5. Writing a Minute	61
6. A Minute is an Explication	71
7. AVP is Another Gathering Circle	77
8. Change and Transformation	97
9. AVP is an Adaptive Process	105
10. The Future of Quaker Practice	109
References	117
About the Author	119

1. INTRODUCTION

Here in this work we will explore some social implications of Eugene Gendlin's Philosophy of the Implicit. We will do that by crossing Gendlin's experiential concept of the Implicit with how the Religious Society of Friends (Quakers) organize around seeking what they call the "Light Within". We will use Quaker practices to understand how the Implicit functions in a group setting.

If you are approaching this work with a background in studying Gendlin's philosophy, my hope is that in exploring Quaker practices you will gain an understanding of how the Implicit functions in a group setting. If you are a reader with experience as a Quaker and with knowledge of Gendlin's work, my hope is that you will find how the language of Quakers and Gendlin's language cross and can inform and deepen our understanding of both practices. Alternatively, if you are approaching this work as a Quaker (or someone) without any prior exposure to Gendlin, you likely will have to expend some time and effort to understand Gendlin's language. My hope, of course, is that you will find in Gendlin's work a new way of expressing your experiences of sitting in silent meeting and living your Quaker practice. As a friend remarked, "we modern Quakers are stuck in using 17th century Quaker writers to express our experiences in meeting". Gendlin offers a new way of looking at our Quaker experiences.

In Section 2. Getting Started we will set out a few of Gendlin's basic philosophic concepts. Gendlin's work is experiential much in the same way that the Quaker practice of sitting in silent meeting is experiential. Gendlin's concepts say what they are about and are available to us to understand from and out of our own life experiencing. After getting started we will add additional terms and concepts from Gendlin's work as the need arises in the sections that follow

In Section 3. Quaker Practice we describe the Friend's silent meeting as it is practiced in the US and the UK. We set out that the environment that the Quakers have created is a *gathering circle* where change and transformations can take place. We show how Gendlin's key concept of a bodily *felt sense* crosses with the change and transformations that Quakers can and do experience in sitting in meeting. In Section 4. An Underlying Social Process we travel over the same ground, looking at how the meeting unfolds from an implicit process point of view. We explore how the silence flows in a meeting, how speaking in meeting resonates in and between members and can carry the whole meeting forward to a climax. This climax is the "gathered meeting". In process terms we find that this meeting climax is a *felt shift* experienced by the members and the meeting as a whole.

After looking at the silent meeting, we turn our attention in Section 5. Writing A Minute to the Quaker monthly meeting for business. We describe the monthly meeting for business by focusing on the way Quakers make decisions by arriving at a "sense of the meeting", then writing a minute of that decision. Again, we traverse the same ground from an implicit point of view in Section 6. A Minute Is An Explication. There we develop the implicit concept of *explication* to show that reaching a decision by writing a minute leads to the understanding that this Quaker business practice is a *group explication process*. This process lets members arrive at a shared sense of meaning, and a sense of unity in their decisions.

From the business meeting we move on to look at the Alternatives to Violence Project (AVP). In Section 7. AVP Is Another Gathering Circle we take up the history of New York Quakers developing AVP workshops to facilitate non-violence in US prisons in the 1970's. The Quakers modified their gathering circle to facilitate change and transformation in and with inmate participants. We describe the AVP workshop in detail. Because the AVP circle is more *explicit* and *structured* we have more information on how the gathering circle functions. Further, since AVP facilitators take notes and write reports on their workshops, we have yet more information on how change and transformation takes place within and as a result of the workshops. Section 8. Change And Transformation shows the effects of the AVP workshops as reported by inmate participants and by observations from AVP facilitators.

After looking at the AVP workshop, in Section 9. AVP Is An Adaptive Process we look at how the Quakers adapted the gathering circle to fit the needs of working with prison inmates. We look at the key changes, which they made to make the circle: more *explicit*; more *active;* and more *struc-*

tured. From an implicit point of view, we have conceptualized this process as an *adaptive process.*

Finally, in a brief epilogue in Section 10. The Future Of Quaker Practice we look at the factors that have contributed to the decline of silent meetings in the US and the UK. We suggest what we gained in an understanding of Quaker practices by viewing the meeting's gathering circle and the adapted AVP gathering circle from an implicit point of view. And further, we look at what we have gained in understanding how the Implicit functions in a group setting. Here we are indebted to the long history of the Quakers in writing about their meetings for worship and their monthly meetings for business. We are especially indebted to the early Quakers who wrote in detail about their seeking after the "Truth".

2. GETTING STARTED

Gendlin's Philosophy of the Implicit is contained in several volumes and essays, but his most comprehensive work is given in *A Process Model*.[1] His philosophy conceptualizes our living as a process. It provides a model both for understanding how we are living, and for thinking *further* about how we are living. Both the concepts and conceptualizing are part of the same process. One way of thinking about Gendlin's work is that he presents us with an "open source philosophy".[2] The term Implicit comes from Gendlin's basic concept of "occurring into implying", which we set out below.

Experiencing

Experiencing is concrete.[3] It is what we feel inside when we say I am feeling "this" way. We are self-aware of "this" feeling. We can turn our attention to it at any given moment. It is not fixed. It is not made up of discrete units. Our experiencing is more rich and intricate than we conceptualize. It is always "more" than we can differentiate.[4]

Occurring into Implying

Experiencing is interacting. We are constantly self-locating and self-registering with our physical and social environment. Consider that you have a feeling sense of what is behind you.

Try closing your eyes and sensing what is behind you.

Open your eyes. Try to recall your experience. Then read on.

---

[1] Eugene Gendlin, *A Process Model*, Northwestern University Press, 2018. Abbreviated as *APM*. I use the terms "Philosophy of the Implicit" and "Process Model" interchangeably.

[2] I am indebted to Elliot Trapp for the phrase "open source philosophy".

[3] Eugene Gendlin, *Experiencing and the Creation of Meaning*, Northwestern University Press, 1997, p.6. Abbreviated as *ECM*.

[4] *APM*, pp. 9-13.

Each event (interacting) in a living process implies a further step. Each event is an occurring into an implying. In the example above in turning your attention to your sensing of what was behind you, your implying (some next step) likely led you to want to turn and visually verify what you were sensing. If you are in familiar surroundings, this wanting may only have been fleeting, and you may have just glanced (after you opened your eyes) to confirm your surroundings. If you are in unfamiliar surroundings, you may have turned your head to verify what was behind you.[5]

In each interacting, we imply our next step. Our next step is implicit. It is *some* step, but it is not explicit. It only becomes explicit when we interact with our environment, with others, or with ourselves. Gendlin often uses hunger as a first teaching example of what he means by implying. Say we are experiencing hunger, we may take it as implying feeding, as implying feeding as a next step. But hunger is *not* hidden feeding. Normally we would think of eating food as implied by hunger. Say, however, we eat some bad food, throw up and do not digest. Our hunger is paused, but still implied. Our implying may be for just resting for a while, not eating immediately. After some time we may feel hungry and eat again. Or in another real world case, some other feeding, like an IV feeding could occur into hunger. Implying only implies some way forward. Occurring is not predetermined. When feeding occurs into hunger, the hunger is satisfied and changed into a new implying.[6]

The key point that Gendlin makes with occurring into implying is that we (or any living process) imply our own change.

The Felt Sense and Felt Shift

Gendlin's philosophy is a philosophy of our (or any) living process. It is experiential. It is bodily sensed. If our implying carries forward (when we take an explicit step in an interaction), our implying changes into a *new* implying of some next step. We experience this change in implying as a feeling process. Occurring into implying are not separate events. When we are in a situation, say as we are seeking to find meaning in our situation, we have a

---

[5] *APM*, p. 106. In this example our feeling sense is the feeling of what we term "perception". Here it is a self-locating sense of our situation. It is a single sequence of both feeling and perception.

[6] *APM*, pp. 9-11. See also *APM*, Note 9, p. 263.

vague bodily sense in our seeking. As we find words that fit our sense of the situation we experience a sense of the rightness of the fit. We say, "We have a felt sense of the situation." We have a formed felt sense of the meaning that we are seeking. As we express our meaning with the words that come to us we have a feeling sense of carrying forward. As our words expressing our meaning carry us forward, we experience this carrying forward as a bodily sensed shift. We say, "We have experienced a felt shift in our situation". The whole of our living situation is carried forward. If we were stuck in our seeking, we sense our becoming unstuck as a felt shift.

Quakers are called Quakers because when Quakers rose to speak in a meeting they often trembled and quaked when they spoke. The Quaker practice of sitting in silent meeting and rising to speak is a bodily felt and bodily sensed process, a deeply felt and deeply expressed speaking. Quakers sought to find a quiet inner space and wait upon what they call the "Light within" to lead them in their speaking.

Focusing

Gene Gendlin viewed forming a felt sense as a natural process. However, we moderns often have trouble letting a bodily felt sense form. To aid finding a felt sense, Gendlin developed a step-by-step process to help people come to experience a bodily felt sense of a situation. Gendlin gave the name "Focusing" to this practice.[7] Focusing grew in part from Gendlin's experiences early on as a young man sitting in silent meeting in Pendle Hill, PA. Focusing shares a "commonality" with the deep bodily knowing that arises in Quaker meeting. Looking back on his experience of sitting in silent meeting and his Focusing work, Gendlin commented:

Focusing arises from within a deep tradition that Quakers preserve for the world.[8]

In one sense, with this text I am bringing the fruits of Gendlin's philosophical and Focusing work back to Quakers and the Quaker meeting, bringing his work back to an early source of his philosophical insights.

---

[7] Eugene Gendlin, *Focusing*, Bantam Books (2nd Ed.), 1981.
[8] Nancy Saunders "Focusing on the Light", in *Seeing, Hearing, Knowing*, John Lampen (Ed.), Sessions, 2008, p.37.

Next

Let's turn then to look at the long-standing Quaker practice of sitting in silent meeting. We will seek to understand this Quaker practice in terms of occurring into implying, and a felt sense and felt shift.

3. QUAKER PRACTICE

The Quaker Practice of holding a silent meeting for worship has persisted for over 350 years since its rise in the northwest of England. Led by George Fox the early Quakers called themselves "Friends of the Truth" and set out a practice of seeking what they called the "Light within".

Quakers met and continue to meet on First Day (Sunday) for worship. Here we will examine the silent (unprogrammed) meeting that arose with George Fox and other early ministers.[1] This is the modern common form of meeting in the UK, and one of two meeting types in the US.[2] Quakers meet for worship in what is called a "meetinghouse", the Quaker term for a church. The meetinghouse usually is a simple, unadorned building. Often in the US the building has been converted from some prior use. Inside the meetinghouse the meeting's chairs are set out in a circle. If the space is small, or if the meeting is large, the chairs may be set out in two or three concentric circles.[3]

Meeting in small groups in silent worship, waiting on the light, we have only the barest of instructions from George Fox setting out what Quaker practice is during worship:

> *Be still and cool in your own mind and spirit from your own thoughts, and you will then feel the divine source of life in you turn your mind to the Lord God. And in doing this you will receive his strength and life-giving power to quieten every storm and gale which blows against you... When the light discloses and reveals things to you, things that tempt you, that confuse*

---

[1] This early group of ministers often was called the "Valiant Sixty".
[2] The second type is a pastoral (programmed) meeting. The split in the US meetings occurred in the mid-1800's. The pastoral meetings have a pastor, hymns and an evangelical-type service.
[3] In some older meetings a "facing bench" for elders sits facing the circle, making the circle into an oval with a cut off end.

> *you, distract you and the like, don't go looking at them, but look at the light that has made you aware of them. And with this same light you will feel yourself rising above them and empowered to resist them... That enables you to overcome them, and you will find grace and strength. And that is the first step to peace. [George Fox, 1658]*[4]

Silent Meeting

Before the start time of the meeting for worship, a person will come in and sit in silence. One or two others also may enter and sit in silence. They may take chairs spacing themselves in the circle. As the start of the hour approaches and more people enter, the meeting room already is filled with a welcoming silence. Again this practice of preparing the meeting dates from the early days. Here is a letter from an early friend giving this advice:

> *The first that enters into the place of your meeting ... turn in thy mind to the light, and wait upon God singly, as if none were present but the Lord; and here thou art strong. Then the next that comes in, let them in simplicity of heart sit down and turn to the same light, and wait in the spirit; so all the rest coming in, in the fear of the Lord, sit down in pure stillness and silence of all flesh, and wait in the light ... In such a meeting there will be an unwillingness to part asunder, being ready to say in yourselves, it is good to be here: and this is the end of all words and writings to bring people to the eternal living Word. [Alexander Parker, 1660].*[5]

After the meeting has settled in a deep silence, which usually takes fifteen or twenty minutes, a member may rise to speak. She may speak on an issue she is dealing with in her life, or she may speak about an issue that affects the meeting as a whole. She may say that "she has been waiting in the light", or that she has been "holding her concern in the light". Further,

---

[4] Modern translation by Rex Ambler, *Light to live by*, Quaker Books, 2002, p. 20. Abbreviated as *Ltlb*.

[5] Rex Ambler, *The Quaker Way*, Christian Alternative Books, 2013, pp. 58-59. Abbreviated as TQW.

she may say that she felt God's presence, or a divine presence while working through her situation to speak. After some silence others may rise to speak. If a member's speaking calls for an action in her own life or in the life of the meeting, Quakers call such speaking a "leading". Allowing for silence between speaking is integral to the meeting so that the members may sit with what has been said.[6] Other speakers may follow, developing the same theme. Or, they too may raise concerns that they have "held in the light". In meetings where there are frequent visitors who likely are unfamiliar with Quaker ways, the meeting may hand out small placards suggesting that visitors test their own desires to speak by asking if what they contemplate saying is relevant to others in the meeting, and asking also that they allow for and respect the silence between speakers.

About fifteen minutes before the end of the hour's meeting children from First Day (Sunday) School may enter and join their parents, usually sitting on the floor beside their parent's chairs. The meeting clerk seated in the circle signals the end of the meeting by shaking hands with those nearest to him or her. Handshakes move around the circle. The clerk may then ask for visitors or newcomers to introduce themselves. After the visitors are welcomed the clerk may make some meeting announcements, then stand to signal the "rise of meeting". The meeting often offers refreshments and the members may then socialize before departing the meetinghouse.

A Modern View

Why do Quakers persist in meeting and speaking in silence in this way? Rex Ambler, a contemporary English Quaker who has led a movement to deepen the spiritual life of Quakers in the UK, sets out an answer:

> *Quakers sit in silence because they want to know something that words cannot tell them. They want to feel something or become aware of something so that they can really make a connection with it. It is something fundamental to their life, they know that, indeed it is the underlying reality of their life, but they normally are not aware of it. They are preoccupied with other things. They are taken up, like others, with the relatively*

---

[6] Advice for meeting practices is given in Faith and Practice, which is usually published by a Yearly Meeting for its member monthly meetings.

> *shallow things of life, encouraged by the media and culture generally, and they hardly feel the depth of it all. So they feel the loss, the distance, and want somehow to get closer to this deeper reality. They want to become 'Friends of the Truth', as they liked to call themselves at the beginning. Not any truth, but the truth that relates specifically to their deepest felt needs, and the needs of the world. They are looking for a truth by which to live, that is, a sense of reality that tells them who they are and how they should live. They want the truth in this sense because that is the only basis on which they could expect to enjoy life to the full and to contribute to life. Part of their life, of course, is their relationship with one another and other people, both near and far. So they want to 'discern' what happens between people, what makes a good life together, and what makes for a bad one. They want to learn on their own experience how relationships that are broken can be mended, how conflicts can be resolved, and how the 'Friends of the Truth' can work together to make things happen in the world.[7]*

Rex Ambler's notion of truth here is not our modern concept of scientific truth with its reliance on facts and proofs. Rather it points to an earlier experiential truth that animated the expressions of the early Quakers. It is a spiritual truth. Our own modern reliance on scientific truth diminishes and pushes aside this understanding of a wider more deep-seated truth in our living. Still the need for something wider to guide our living in and with the members of a meeting and beyond remains, and is, if anything, more keenly needed in our modern times.

The Experience

Whether from earlier times or now in modern times, the Quaker experience of sitting together in silent meeting is *to get beyond words*, to get to a place or space that is open, that leads to an *opening*. Speakers when they rise, speak from *that* opening. Their speaking is deeply *bodily felt*. In earlier times Friends often trembled and quaked when they spoke. (As we have

---

[7] Rex Ambler, *TQW*, p.11.

suggested the term Quaker comes from the quaking that accompanied early Friends' speaking.)

Rufus Jones, a Quaker leader in the last century describes a woman rising to speak in his boyhood meeting in rural Maine:

> *At the head of the upper row of women Friends sat a woman of unusual grace and dignity. She wore a bonnet of the usual Quaker type; underneath it a white muslin cap, and over her shoulders a neatly folded silk scarf or shawl. One could see that she was becoming **tremulous**, and I knew in advance that she was being inwardly '**moved**' to rise with a message. The first visible sign was the untying of her silk bonnet strings, then the graceful removal of her bonnet, which she passed to her nearest companion... Then she arose to her full height ... Her voice was soft like the wind in pine trees, but with a cadence and a carrying power which reached every listener. There was a slight change of position on the part of the listeners, and all turned to the woman who had arisen. She began in a whisper, but we all heard every word... 'He brought me to His banqueting house and the banner over me was love.' The amazing, seeking, pursuing love of God was ... her theme ... with a mounting voice – still clear as a bell – she described the glories of the heavenly city... As she sat down and put on her bonnet and tied its strings, a deep hush spread over us and the canopy of love became a real covering.* [8]

When a speaker rises to speak in this deeply felt way her speaking *resonates* with the other members present. They too may feel their bodies respond in an empathetic way, nod their heads in agreement and feel some forward movement in their own lives as they settle back into the meeting's silence.

No Beliefs

The meeting experience of speaking and listening to others speak is central to Quaker practice. Quakers are almost unique among western reli-

---

[8] Jessamyn West, *The Quaker Reader,* Pendle Hill Publications, 1962, pp. 419-420. ***My emphasis.***

gious groups in not requiring, or even advocating a set of beliefs.[9] All their practice points to the *how* to get to the meeting experience, not the *what*. Often, they may view words describing beliefs as a hindrance to gaining their own experience, rather than as a help. What Quakers say or do follows from their direct experience. Their focus is on *right living*.

What early Quakers learned and later Quakers have affirmed is that in sitting and waiting, their needs and the needs of the world will be met. As Rex Ambler suggests,

> *So, what Fox discovered… is that you can make contact with the deep reality of your life, and that it is responsive to your need and the need of the world.*[10]

If you wait patiently in the light, the *right* words will come to you to speak and, if not then, some time after a *leading* may come showing you a way forward, a way of living forward. There is no ritual here; no set of beliefs that will produce some desired result. Rather, the only pointer here is the *light*. In Fox's time the light referred to the "light of conscience", or more commonly the "light of Jesus Christ". As Christianity has receded among meetings the term "light" has acquired a broader, if lessened metaphorical meaning of seeing more deeply into your life and what ways may lay before you.

Testimonies

Throughout their history Quakers have engaged in the world, beginning with George Fox admonishing Friends in their ministry:

> *Be patterns, be examples in all countries, places, islands, nations, wherever you come, that your carriage and life may preach among all sorts of people, and to them. Then you will come to walk cheerfully over the world, answering that of God in every one, whereby in them ye may be a blessing and make the witness of God in them bless you. [George Fox, 1656]*[11]

---

[9] The Universalist Unitarians also are an exception.
[10] Rex Ambler, *TQW*, p. 21.
[11] *TQW*, p. 109.

The Quaker practice is to live your life out of your own experience of the *light within*, to go with a *leading* that comes to you. The *what* that you take away from your sitting in meeting is the way you choose to live your life – not saying just words, but acting in the particulars that guide your life. What Quakers have learned is that if you follow in this Quaker path; you will be led to what are called "testimonies". These are not beliefs; rather they are the accumulated witnessing of individual Quakers and meetings, an accumulated history of living by example. The testimonies are not beliefs, but a call to live in *harmony* with your experience.

The four traditional Quaker testimonies given in each *Faith and Practice* are: Equality, Simplicity, Honesty, and Peace.[12]

Equality simply means to treat each and all persons the same. In the early days in England with rigid social castes Quakers paid a steep prison price for not doffing their hats, or bowing to nobility. In the US, Quakers were active in the movement to free slaves, and later in the vanguard of the Civil Rights Movement in the 1960's in the south.

Simplicity means attending to your needs in and with a simple life-style so that you can attend to the needs of others. Simplicity in our modern times is completely at variance with our media driven consumer life-style.

Honesty means speaking the truth at all times. Again early Quakers paid a steep price to keep this testimony. They refused to take an oath in court proceedings, saying quite rightly that they spoke the truth at all times and made no exceptions. We owe our Quaker predecessors for our right to affirm that we will tell the truth in court and not take a bible oath. The same commitment to honesty led Quaker merchants to choose a fair price, a "fixed" price, for goods and to offer it to all customers. Again this is something we now take for granted.

Peace means no inward and outward violence. Peace is likely the best known of the Quaker testimonies. Quakers have been against wars since their beginnings in England. They have registered as "conscientious objectors" in our modern wars, and served in non-combatant roles in hospitals

---

[12] In the UK and the US more modern expressions of the four testimonies are often used. In the UK they are phrased as: Equality and Justice, Peace, Truth and Integrity, and Simplicity and Sustainability. See www.quaker.org.uk/about-quakers/our-values. Personal communication from Helen Meads.

and ambulance corps as well as in an alternative service like the American Friends Service Committee, caring for refugees in the two World Wars.

It is easy to list these simple testimonies, but they are hard to live by. Each Quaker needs the support of his or her meeting when making life decisions, especially decisions involving social actions that may place the person or his or her family at risk. When a leading arises for a Quaker often his or her first response it to *test* the leading with members of the meeting. Quakers have learned to form what are called "Clearness Committees"[13]. These committees often help a member test his or her leading. This help is done with gentle questioning by the committee members, looking at the strength and commitment of a proposed course of action. For example, asking the person if she or he has thought through and considered the consequences of what she or he proposes to do. There is no rush. The committee may meet several times until all have a sense that the member is *clear* about what he or she proposes to do. If no *clearness* is reached, the member may be asked to give further thought (seasoning) to what actions she or he proposes to take. Generally, the matter is carried through until the member and the committee are clear about a course of action.

Experiment with Light

Given the fact that Quaker meetings provide no formal instruction in how to sit in silent meeting, it is not surprising that the number of Quakers has and is declining in the UK and the US. In earlier times meetings were stable, especially in rural farming communities. Families knew one another. Children growing up attending meetings ("birthright" Quakers) spent their time into their early teens observing and listening to adults in the meeting. They simply absorbed how to approach and sit in meeting with family conversations often as their only guide.

In our modern times with the frequent movement of work and families, much of that continuity and time together is lost. Meetings are urban and suburban. Most Quakers today have joined their meeting at some time later in life. They are "convinced" Quakers. Many are drawn to meeting by the Quakers commitment to social actions. However, many social activ-

---

[13] A Clearness Committee usually has three of four members. These committees are formed to help a member work through a variety of difficult life situations not just social actions. These are situations like marriage, divorce or changing work.

ists struggle to understand how meeting works, especially the silences and deep listening that meeting requires. Meetings often become what old-timers call "popcorn" meetings where attenders tend to "pop off" about the latest social injustice, often in rapid fire without any intervening silence.

With the current beleaguered state of many meetings as a background, Rex Ambler, a UK Quaker and scholar studying George Fox's writings, set out to try to understand how Fox and the early Quakers experienced what they reported from their sitting together. Ambler was then editing an extensive anthology of George Fox's Journal and letters called *Truth of the Heart*.[14] He was driven by his need to understand more deeply what Fox was saying and by a spiritual crisis in his own life that he was unable to resolve.[15] After some trial and error Ambler was able to construct a four-step meditation from Fox's early writings:[16]

> *Mind the Light*
>
> *Open your heart to the Truth*
>
> *Wait in the Light.*
>
> *Submit to the Truth.*

Ambler chose each step from a passage from George Fox. For example, the first step "Mind the Light" comes from the following passage:

> *Mind the pure light of God in you, which shows you sin and evil, and how you have spent your time, and shows you how your minds go forth. [George Fox, 1654]*[17]

Ambler began to use these four steps as a meditative practice, which he called an "experiment with light". He set aside a half hour each day to meditate. After some time he was able to reach a point, an *opening*, where he resolved the personal relationships that had plagued him as a spiritual crisis. The process worked. He attained a sense of peace and freedom to act in his relationships. Later he described his experience to a psychother-

---

[14] Rex Ambler, *Truth of the Heart*, Quaker Books, 2001. Abbreviated TotH.
[15] Rex Ambler, *Ltlb*, pp. 2-3.
[16] Ltlb, pp. 16-22. See also Harbert Rice, *Language Process Notes,* Focusing Institute, 2008, p. 54.
[17] *Ltlb*, pp. 16-17.

apist friend. She remarked that his four-step meditation was quite similar to a six-step process, called *Focusing,* that Eugene Gendlin had worked out to help people come to a bodily felt sense of a situation. She recommended that Ambler get a copy of Gendlin's book on Focusing.[18]

Focusing is usually taught and practiced in pairs with one person acting as a listener while the other focuses, saying what he or she is feeling while working through the six-step process. They then switch roles and the listener becomes the focuser. Ambler found that after reading Gendlin's book he could focus without having a partner as a listener. Much to his surprise he found he could come to the same place that he had found with his light meditation. He could take Focusing to a deep place, reaching the same space that he did with his light meditation.

Moreover, Ambler liked the way that the initial Focusing steps made it easier to get past the cacophony of thoughts that swirl around when a person tries to reach a stillness that allows them to focus on a single concern or issue. Expressed in Quaker terms this is the process of *centering down*. When focusing, Ambler called it "focusing down".

His experiences with Focusing led Ambler to modify his four-step meditation into a six-step meditation incorporating elements of Focusing.[19]

Crossing with Focusing

In effect Rex Ambler had crossed his Light Meditation with Focusing. Here is the early six-step process that he called an "Experiment with Light":

> **Relax body and mind...** *Let yourself become wholly receptive. In this receptive state of mind,* **let the real concerns of your life emerge.** *Ask yourself, 'What is really going on in my life?'... but do not try to answer the question ...*
>
> *Now* **focus on one issue** *that presents itself, one thing that gives you a sense of unease. And try to get a sense of this thing as a whole...*

---

[18] Eugene Gendlin, *Focusing*, Bantam Books, 2nd Edition, 1981. Here the process of letting a felt sense form has come full circle: moving from Gendlin's insight for Focusing in sitting in Quaker Meeting round to aid Rex Ambler in working out a step-by-step process from George Fox's writings.

[19] Rex Ambler, *Ltlb*, pp. 37-38.

> *Now ask yourself **why is it like that**... Wait in the light till you see what it is. Let the answer come.*
>
> *When the answer comes **welcome it**... Trust the light. Say yes to it. Submit to it... It will show you the way through.*
>
> *As soon as you accept what is being revealed to you, you will begin to **feel different**... Accepting truth about your self is like making peace.*

Ambler first presented this meditation at a General Meeting of Friends in England in 1996. He taught his "Experiment with Light" to 120 members as a guided meditation. The Friends response was immediate:

> *The result at that meeting of Friends was tangible. It was evident from their faces, many of them with tears, that some of them had been deeply affected. Others stood up to say that they had gained insight or clarity on an issue that greatly concerned them. They asked if we could meet again in the free time and do the meditation once more, this time with space to share our experiences more fully. So after lunch 34 Friends met in a crowded loft and we went through the six-step process once again. One or two were clearly having difficulty, but most of them gained something of real value.*[20]

Rex Ambler himself was deeply moved by his experience with the Friends response to his Light Meditation. He comments:

> *As I walked home from that meeting, I realized that I had to devote myself to this work. It was possible to teach this practice, it **did** help people to open to the light, and, surprisingly, they could help one another to understand it.*[21]

Having resolved to teach the practice, Ambler spent the next three years tirelessly traveling in the UK and Europe, teaching the practice as a guided meditation and forming what are called "Light Groups" in meet-

---

[20] *Ltlb*, p. 38.
[21] *Ltlb*, p. 39. ***Ambler's emphasis***

ings. The practice evolved into a guided meditation taking about 40 minutes. Afterwards the members would journal and share their experiences. As Ambler noted early on, members who took easily to the meditation could help to teach others. Some who adopted the meditation, carried it over as their sitting practice in meeting, focusing on concerns and issues affecting the meeting. Light Groups have led to a rekindling of the spirit among UK Quaker silent meetings.

When he published *Light to live by* in 2003 Rex Ambler estimated that there were some sixty Light groups.[22] Since Ambler's early work establishing Light Groups, the practice has evolved and spread. By 2018 there were over 100 Light Groups. Most of these groups were in the UK. As Rex Ambler stepped back a small group of Friends organized the Experiment with Light Network. Britain Yearly Meeting (BYM) recognizes the Light Network organization.[23] The Network publishes a journal and helps organize and sustain Light groups.[24] As the Light groups have evolved the texts used in meditation have evolved as well. While Rex Ambler's early meditation retained some focusing influence, the Light meditation texts have evolved independently of Focusing. Some groups have chosen to use Ambler's early Quaker four-step mediation. Others have developed their own texts.[25] Forming Light groups responds to a need among Friends to deepen the spiritual life of meetings. Some groups form and last a few seasons; others have sustained their members and meetings for more than ten years. The interest and practice still centers in the UK. Light groups in North America have not formed their own organization. Rather they work with the Light Network in the UK. The lesser interest and practice of the Experiment with Light in the US may simply reflect the fact that the US up to now has not seen a tireless early advocate for the meditation like Rex Ambler.

Underlying Language Process

With the understanding that both Light Meditation and Focusing can and do lead to a bodily felt sense of a situation, we can begin to explore

---

[22] *Ltlb*, p.60.
[23] BYM has a category of "Quaker Recognised Body". The Experiment with Light Network was recognized by the BYM's Meeting for Suffering in 2017.
[24] www.experiment-with-light.org.uk
[25] For example, see John Lampen (Ed.), *Seeing, Hearing, Knowing, Reflections on Experiment with Light, Sessions,* 2008.

Quaker practices from the point of view of Gendlin's Philosophy of the Implicit.

Here are the Quaker and Focusing language sequences that can and often do lead to a bodily felt sense:

Language Sequences that Can Lead to a Felt Sense[26]

Quakers	Focusing
Mind the Light	Clearing a Space
Relax body and mind...	*What wants my awareness?*
Question	Felt Sense
What is going on in my life? Or, What is going on in my Meeting?	*Sense what comes...*
Open Your Heart	Get a Handle
Focus on one concern...	*What is the feeling quality of the felt sense?*
Wait in the Light	Resonate
Why is it like that?	*Go back and forth between the quality word and the felt sense. Is that right?*
Truth	Ask
Welcome the truth...	*What does it need? Or, what does it want me to know?*
Reflect	Receive
Consider how you need to act...	*Welcome what comes...*

Turning Inward and Questioning

When I look at these language sequences I often think of geese flying off from a pond. If you have seen geese taking off, you have seen they must

---

[26] These Language Sequences are from Harbert Rice, *Language Process Notes*, Focusing Institute, 2008, p. 52. I have modified that last Light Meditation step to focus on the Quaker meeting (group) emphasis on social engagement. See Rex Ambler's group meditation in *Ltlb*, p.49.

take several running steps on the surface of the pond before they become airborne. For us these sequences of sayings are steps that help us get to an inner space where a felt sense may form.

The first of the steps help us to turn inward and get past the "cacophony" of thoughts that swirl around us, the shoulds, have to's, and need to's that we perpetually carry around with us. What we inwardly seek is that "still point in the turning world".[27] We want that still point where we can set ourselves at ease and bodily sense our situation.

We try to get a sense of our situation by questioning.[28] For Quakers this questioning is asking, "What is going on in my life?" Or, "What is going on in my meeting? In Focusing, the initial questioning often is "What wants my awareness?

Following this initial questioning, both practices look for a response. For Quakers, the looked-for response is the "Truth". In Focusing it is the forming of the "felt sense". We find a name by bodily feeling a resonating as we search and try different words until we find a fit. In both saying sequences we have a common language pattern calling for an inward turning, a questioning, and an expecting a response.

If it comes, the response is the forming of a felt sense. We cannot say what will come. A felt sense forms as it can form. We only know the forming after the event. The response we encounter may not be simple. A forming felt sense is a singular event. It may take us some time to work it out. Or, it may take us several sessions if a felt sense forms over time.

Finding a Felt Sense Is a Natural Process

Gendlin emphasizes that finding a felt sense is a natural process. He developed his Focusing steps to facilitate this natural process. In addition, he suggests that this turning inward and questioning is aided when we interact with a partner, another person who listens and empathizes with our seeking a felt sense. In the same way, the Light Meditation steps created by Rex Ambler offer an alternative set of steps to facilitate forming a felt sense. The Experiment with Light meditation as it has developed among

---

[27] T.S. Eliot's phrase from the *Four Quartets*.
[28] For Quakers this is another form of seeking a response by questioning. Quakers call this questioning practice "Queries".

Quakers is practiced as a group meditation. Again, the process of forming a felt sense is enhanced by the group interactions that follow as members share their responses of what came to them in the meditation.[29] This natural forming of a felt sense may explain why early Quakers felt no need to formalize steps in their inward seeking. Early Quakers spent long hours together "minding the light". They were not time-limited in the way that we moderns are. When "truth" came to early Quakers, it came as it would come with long, patient waiting and the support of fellow "seekers".

Interacting – Life Carrying Forward

Now if we look again at these language sequences from an Implicit point of view we see we have an interaction, or more precisely a sequence of interactions. We experience our meditation or focusing as a feeling process, a bodily sensed process. If our implying carries forward in an occurring (when we take an explicit step), our implying changes into a *new* implying of some next step. We experience this change in implying as a feeling process. Here in our meditation (or focusing) each of our next steps is a freshly forming implying. Our implying points to some next step, but a step only comes with an actual occurring. *Each "this step" is a freshly forming implying.* Occurring into implying are not separate events. All occurring occurs into an implying, but not all occurring carries implying forward. The primary distinction is between those interactions (events) that carry life forward and those that do not.[30] We experience the sequence of occurring changes in our implying as a feeling process of continuity.[31] We experience our own changing as carrying our living forward.

Crossing Everything-by-Everything

How then do we imply our own change? Gendlin gives us a way to think further about implying and our own change: *eveing*.[32]

---

[29] The group sharing following meditation takes a particular Quaker form called "worship sharing". See http://www.experiment-with-light.org.uk/holding-lg.pdf, pp. 6-8.

[30] We have a bodily felt sense of the difference. When our interactions carry us forward, we experience a sense of aliveness. When our interactions fail to carry us forward, we often experience a sense that we are stuck.

[31] *APM*, pp. 67-70.

[32] *APM*, pp. 41-42.

Eveing stands for *everything-by-everything*. Each implying forms freshly. Gendlin calls a freshly forming implying an eveing.

I think the easiest way to understand eveing is to think about how differences in our past experiences are brought forward and *crossed* with differences in future ways forward for us. We don't know what aspects of our past experiences are relevant in our situation until a felt sense forms, and we don't know what way will carry us forward until a felt sense forms. Each implying is already all the differences made to each other as a way forward, as a way of carrying our living forward. An eveing is all the differences made to each other as they *interaffect* each other.[33]

For me, *crossing* is an easier way of thinking about how differences in our past experiences and differences in future ways forward interaffect each other and the whole.[34] We can say, for example, that crossing *opens* our past experiences, as aspects of all our experiences and makes them relevant in the present situation, in the present occurring into implying. Further, occurring into implying crosses our newly relevant past experiences with all possible ways that *can* happen as a way forward.[35] In this sense, an eveing crosses everything-by-everything.[36] Moreover, we sense this implying (of everything-by-everything) as "coming to us" as a whole. Implying (eveing) takes *no time*.[37]

With What Are We Interacting?

Clearly we have an interacting here in our meditation and focusing, in our questioning and a waiting for a response. How is *this* questioning different than any other questioning we might make? With *what* are we interacting?

---

[33] *APM*, pp. 23-24. Gendlin often creates his own terms, here in "eveing", when no common terms can say what he means. We experience the multiplicity of differences in eveing as a whole. Occurring into implying differentiates and redetermines the whole into a new whole. Note Gendlin only speaks of differences, not parts. We only know the parts of our implying after our interaction, after occurring into implying.

[34] *APM*, pp. 30.

[35] Can in this instance is determined only in an occurring. Gendlin in his law of occurrence says "what could occur at a given juncture, did". We can only know the "could" after the (occurring) event (the "did"). *APM*, pp.50-51.

[36] *APM*, p. 42.

[37] *APM*, p. 51.

Let me lay out an answer:

When we question in this way, we are interacting with our own implying.

Now, let us explore further the implications that follow from this answer.

Getting Beyond Words

What happens when we interact with our own implying? How do we think about a felt sense forming? And how do we think about a felt shift that arises with a formed felt sense?

Clearly we have something new here. We get beyond words in our familiar patterns of speaking. When we form a felt sense we create a new environment, a new space[38]. Expressed in Quaker terms this is an *opening, or more precisely an opening of a way forward.*

When we get beyond words, beyond our situation for a time however fleeting as a felt sense forms, we experience a life-affirming "Yes! Yes!" moment. We experience a felt shift of release and change. The outward changes we may show can be quite small. The inward changes, however, often are enormous.

When we interact with our own implying we experience life in this new way. The experience is different. In Gendlin's terms, we experience a new feel for the whole of our situation. Our "whole situation" moves forward. If we were stuck, we can come unstuck. Coming unstuck still requires work on our part. While we have a new understanding of our situation, we still have to take steps to say and do what will carry us forward. With a felt sense forming we are living into our own changing, our implying is changed as it implied itself being changed. We carry forward with our bodily felt sense of our next move,[39]

---

[38] Gendlin calls this new environment "Implicit Space". The concept of Implicit Space is laid out in *APM,* Chapter VIII, pp. 198-240. We will explore the idea of Implicit Space in the next section when we look at the underlying social process in the Quaker meeting.

[39] *APM,* p. 212.

Our feeling interaction with our implying is our feeling of change as a whole situation "gels" for us. We get a sense of our life-situation and a way forward. With this opening of a way forward, a new fresh sense of self comes, a new self and a new beginning. This is the change that we "needed" to carry forward.[40] This is the new self and new beginning recounted by Quakers in their quest to "get beyond words".

Leadings as a Direct Referent

Now let us introduce a new implicit term, the Direct Referent. Gendlin uses Direct Referent as an alternate term for a formed felt sense. Direct Referent lets us understand our experience of carrying forward by going back to our experience of a formed felt sense. Unlike our seeking experience in meditation or focusing, we can go directly to our formed felt sense. As we seek to put together words or actions that come from our felt sense, these word and action sequences form freshly in our implying as we carry forward. A Direct Referent is the experience of a felt sense that Quakers call a "leading". For Quakers, responding to a formed felt sense leads to a sense of direction, not any direction but a sense of the "right" direction. Gendlin makes the same point with regards to a formed felt sense, a Direct Referent. When a Direct Referent has formed, we have a feeling sense of "direction".[41] This "direction" has as yet no explicit content, no explicit form, yet we "know" that we have a direction. This direction is still implicit, still yet to unfold. We can say:

> *A Quaker leading is a formed felt sense, a Direct Referent, which*
> *gives a sense of right direction to carry life forward in a new way.*

What then? What do we do after we have a Direct Referent? We have to work it out. We have to live out our leading in our everyday living.

Speaking in a New Way

We live in our everyday world of speaking and acting. We now must work out what to say and do by referring to our experiential reference (Direct Referent), our formed felt sense that brings forth new words and actions. Gendlin calls this working out "second sequences".[42] There can

---

[40] *APM*, p. 213.
[41] *APM*, p. 230. See also ECM, p. 238.
[42] *APM*, p. 225-226. The "first sequence" is the forming of the felt sense (Direct Referent).

be and often is enormous power in words that come from those speaking from such an experience in meeting. Words sound fresh. They are newly formed and resonate with other members. When we speak and act we are interacting with our formed felt sense. We experience our interacting as new, as a sequence of freshly forming occurring's. Each newly forming occurring is a new way forward, a new way following on anew and anew yet again.

How, we might ask, can a single experience, a single instance, change and transform a life and the lives of others?

The answer is:

> *A singular experience of a formed felt sense arising from interacting with our implying applies to everything.*[43]

Everything refers to all the instances, which we may work out by making explicit the second sequences, the sequences of words and actions arising from our Direct Referent. Each time we work out a sequence we carry our life forward. Each instance is in effect a new expression, a new carrying forward. Each instance changes the context in which we live and act, including our interactions with others. Our speaking and acting comes from a sense of freedom, of release from speaking and acting in old ways. When we "touch" a Direct Referent, we again are outside our old life-situation; we can think, act and speak clearly. Words come alive for us and resonate when we speak with others. All of this working out process begins to take place for a Quaker when she begins to *test* a leading by talking with other meeting members, with a Clearness Committee or in meeting itself. Whatever the situation, she comes alive as she describes what she has sensed, what direction she wants to go, what actions she envisions that she must take, or that she envisions that the meeting must undertake.

Holding and Letting

Now we can look more deeply at how change and transformation takes place. While the six word-step sequences that we use in Quaker practice and Focusing seem quite complex, the basic change process is simple and common to each practice.

---

[43] *APM*, p. 226.

> *We can change our lives when we hold a situation and let a felt sense form in a new space, a new opening. Holding and letting is our interacting with our implying. Once a felt sense has formed, we can "work out" what to say or do to further carry our lives forward.*

Holding and letting is one activity, one process.[44] By engaging in our Quaker practice we intend to hold a situation, to keep the point of our concern, problem, or conflict, and let change come as a felt sense forms. This process takes time. It may take a few seconds, or it may take many months.

We say that change *can* come because a felt sense forms only when it forms. Despite our best intentions and our familiarity with our practice, a felt sense may not come, or if it comes it often is not what we expected. Each formed felt sense (Direct Referent) is a singular experience and has its own character.

Saying that holding and letting is one process does not make the process any easier. We live stuck in our old ways of thinking and talking about our situation. It is not easy to hold. Holding means not trying to move forward by speaking words, or acting or even feeling the way we think we "should" act and feel. As soon as we turn inward we turn over the discomfort, pain, fear and disconnect in our lives. Holding often means holding pain. It is easy to turn away and to try to "slide by".

If we hold and let a felt sense form, then we get beyond our situation. We get beyond the words that we have used that failed to carry us forward. Once a felt sense has formed we can speak and act in a new way. All the contexts in our lives have *crossed*, and we have a new reference, a new center. The felt sense is a focused way forward, a new way because we now have a reference "outside" our old situation.

We say we *can* speak and act in a new way. It does not mean that we will. We still live in our everyday patterns of speaking and acting. We still have to work things out. Working out is not easy. We have to say and explain what we are about, and do what we say we are going to do. This is no mere saying or doing. Rather, our Direct Referent leads

---

[44] See *APM*, p. 214.

us to say and act in ways that are new and unique to us in our situation. We experience a Direct Referent as a transforming power as we work out what to say or do.[45] Still, this working out is made easier for us by going back to "touch" our experience of our formed felt sense. Touching also puts us at ease. It is like going back to a cool spring and taking a drink that empowers us again and again to step forward on our new path.

Light and Truth

If holding and letting is the basic process that we seek, how then does occurring into implying map into the Quaker practice of light and truth?

If we "wait in the light" or "turn to the light" or "hold in the light", what we are doing is holding and letting. We are seeking to interact with our implying.

> *Light is implying. Or, we can say "waiting in the light" symbolizes our interacting with our implying.*

In the same way we can say:

> *Truth is what carries life forward. Or, we can say "Truth" symbolizes what comes to us from our implying as we carry life forward. This is a spiritual truth.*

Truth is both implicit and explicit. It is both our on-going implying to carry life forward, and what we say or do explicitly to carry life forward. In this sense, truth is always present for us if we live into it.

Eugene Gendlin makes the same point about implicit/explicit truth. Here is a Quaker-like quote from him:

> *What is true is already so. Owning up to it doesn't make it worse. Not being open to it doesn't make it go away. And because it is true, it is there to be interacted with. Anything untrue isn't there to be lived. People can stand what is true because they are already enduring it.*[46]

---

[45] Transforming Power (TP) is a later Quaker phrase used in Alternatives to Violence (AVP). We shall explore Transforming Power in more detail in Section 7.
[46] Eugene Gendlin, *Focusing*, Bantam Books, 1981, p. 140.

There is always "more" to the truth than we can say or do in any given moment.[47]

Understanding Fox in a New Way

With this understanding (crossing) Quaker "waiting in the light" and Gendlin's holding and letting, we can look again in a modern experiential way at what George Fox is saying:

> *So long as you live in the light nothing can trip you up, because you will see everything in the light. Do you love the light? Then here's your teacher! When you are walking it's there with you, in your heart – you don't have to say 'Look over here,' 'Look over there'. And as you lie in bed it is there with you too, teaching you, making you aware of that wandering mind of yours that likes to wander off, and your attempts to master everything with your own thought and imagination – they themselves are mastered by the light. [George Fox, 1653]*[48]

Now, we can understand why Fox says the "light" is always with us. Our on-going implying is always with us, we have only to turn and wait, the "truth" will come to us; what will carry life forward comes to us. Life itself is our teacher! When we form a felt sense out of our on-going implying, we touch life itself. This felt experiencing does not come from our "wandering mind", rather it comes in and from the "heart". Our living is an embodied process. When we "live in the light" we turn and live into our own implying to change. Each step forward is a turning to, speaking into, and acting into the intricacy of our own implying; there is always "more" to our living, more to come, more to understand, to speak, and to do.

What Have We Gained?

What have we gained by looking at Quaker practice as our experience in forming a felt sense?

---

[47] Saying that light symbolizes implying and truth symbolizes what carries life forward does not preclude, or take away from symbolizing an experience with "light" and "truth" as a religious experience. George Fox and countless Quakers have spoken and written about their experience of the Light within as the "pure light of God".

[48] Rex Ambler's modern translation, *Ltlb*, p.8.

What we have *regained* is a clearer understanding that our living, and our Quaker practice, is an embodied process, an in-the-body-curl-your-toes process. We "quake" because we come alive as we turn and find an opening in implicit space, an opening that leads us to a new self and new way forward. We now can understand how change and transformation comes to us. When we get "beyond words" and form a felt sense, we get beyond our situation and form a new center, a Direct Referent that leads us to speak and act in a changed way. This is our Quaker "leading" expressed in a more precise way as a "working out" how we will speak and act out of and from a Direct Referent.

A Religious Experience

In the same way we gain an understanding of why Quakers can experience a formed felt sense as a religious experience. We easily can understand *occurring* as we speak and act into and out of our implying, but in occurring into implying, implying holds out the "more" in our living. It is beyond our grasp. It is always "more". Gendlin often refers to a felt sense forming at the "edge" of our ordinary awareness. Our experience of a felt sense that arises at this edge is not some altered meditative state. Rather, we are responsive to a felt sense as it forms, as a leading that we seek to follow. Further, as we sit in meeting we experience a felt sense forming as "coming to us". How we choose to express this experience rests with our situation and our past experiences. If we come as Quakers, we may express our experience as waiting upon the "Light within", the "Light of God", or the "Divine". We may experience our sitting as transcendent, as we experience what comes to us as *not ours*. We may then symbolize our experience with those Quaker words and phrases that resonate with our experience of a formed felt sense; and in turn we feel our speaking of what comes to us, the *not ours* resonate with those Friends who are joined with us meeting.

A Responsive Order

Again, we also gain a clear understanding of a question that has long puzzled Quakers. Why when we sit and wait do we get a response? Not all the time, but many times we do get a response – and often the response is often not a response that we sought, or expected.

We get a response because our implying carries all possibilities of our carrying our life forward! Occurring into implying is an ordering process. An implicit order is more intricate and more precise than anything that we can think or say before we experience our formed felt sense. When a felt sense forms, we say, "Ah! That is what I needed". Or, "That is what our meeting needed". We experience our interacting with our implying as a responsive ordering.

Thinking in the Light

Lastly, understanding that the Implicit is an intricate ordering let's us get beyond George Fox's phrase "mastered by the light". Fox is speaking of "mastering" our thinking mind. However, we can do more. We can think in a new way.[49] We can think directly from our own experiencing. Thinking from and out of a felt sense is an explicit embodied way of thinking. Explicitly conceptualizing from and out of a Direct Referent is, in effect, a different way of thinking and a different way of thinking about thinking. We now understand that when we form a Direct Referent, it is a singular event and we regenerate time and (symbol) space relationships. When we think out of and refer to a Direct Referent we "work out" our felt meaning of these changed relationships as they apply to *everything* in our living. When we think in this way, we are both thinking from and out of the intricacy of our own living. In this sense, *as Quakers we can both see and think in the light*.

A Gathered Meeting

So far, we have looked at Quaker Practice (and Focusing) from the point of view of the individual. However, Quaker practice centers on the silent meeting. There is a long Quaker tradition that speaks of the "gathered meeting" or an earlier phrase, the "covered meeting".[50] Thomas R. Kelly, a Quaker mystic from the last century has aptly described the gathered meeting:

> *In the Quaker practice of group worship on the basis of silence come special times when an electric hush and solemnity and depth of power steals over the worshippers. A blanket of divine covering comes over the room, and a quickening Presence*

---

[49] Gendlin calls this type of thinking, "Thinking at the Edge". He along with Mary Hendricks and Kye Nelson worked out a multi-step process to facilitate this type of thinking. See Eugene Gendlin and Mary Hendricks, "Thinking at the Edge: A New Philosophical Practice" in *The Folio*, 2004, Vol. 19, No. 1, pp. 1-24.

[50] I will use the phrases "gathered meeting" and "covered meeting" interchangeably.

pervades us, breaking down some part of the special privacy and isolation of our individual lives and bonding our spirits within a super-individual Life and Power – an objective, dynamic Presence which enfolds us all... and quickens in us depths that had before been slumbering.[51]

From Kelly's description we may infer that a "gathered meeting" occurs as and when it can occur. When gathered, all the members of the meeting, the whole meeting forms a felt sense and experiences a felt shift in their lives. These meetings are rare, and even rarer in our modern meetings. Kelly puts the gathered meeting in perspective:

And as individual mystics who are led deep into the heart of devotion learn to be weaned away from reliance upon special times of vision, learn not to clamor perpetually for the heights but to walk in shadows and valleys and dry places for months and years together, so must group worshippers learn that worship is fully valid when there are no thrills, no special sense of covering... If no blanket of divine covering is warmly felt, and if the wills have been offered together in the silent work of worship, worshippers may still go home content and nourished and say, 'It was a good meeting'.[52]

Next

Next we will turn to look at the silent meeting as an implicit social process.

---

[51] Thomas Kelly, *The Gathered Meeting*, The Tract Association of Friends, 1947, p. 3. This tract is an edited version of a longer essay published in Thomas Kelly, *The Eternal Promise*, Friends United Press, 1977, pp. 47-61.
[52] Thomas Kelly, pp. 19-20.

4. AN UNDERLYING SOCIAL PROCESS

Let's look at how an implicit process unfolds in the Quaker's silent meeting. First, we shall say that this group process creates *an entirely new environment*. Gendlin does not explicitly extend his process model to group processes. So we will be looking to extend implicit concepts to understand the Quaker's silent meeting practice. The silent meeting creates what we shall call a *circles environment*. While there are likely many types of group circles, we will use a new term *gathering circles*, for the Quaker-type circles that we are going to examine.

Establishing a Circle

Why do Quakers meet? Quakers met early on to worship together. Then, during their persecution at the hands of authorities and the established church they met both to worship and to survive. They were not allowed to marry, to bury their dead, and often they were denied work. By meeting together they could support one another and support those among them who were imprisoned. As the persecutions waned, they found that they also needed one another socially.

Why sit in a circle? The circle is an ancient form of group meeting. However, by choosing this form of meeting Quakers explicitly expressed their testimony of equality, and consciously rebuked the religious forms of their day where a minister or priest addressed a congregation from a pulpit or elevated platform. In the Quaker view all members of the meeting are priests! No one is elevated among the members. Even today, the Quaker's meeting's circle stands in stark contrast to the standard form of a western church with its pulpit.[1]

---

[1] A meeting circle was not universal. Some early meetings in the UK show a meeting form where rows of pews face an elder's bench. The Meetinghouses at Farfield (1869) and Coanwood (1760) show this form. Personal communication from Rob Foxcroft,

Besides an expression of equality the Quakers were quite clear that they needed to see one another's faces in meeting. They understood that we need others to mirror back how they see us and to affirm us. The following is the statement that established the first yearly General Meeting of English Friends:

> *We did conclude among ourselves to settle a meeting, to see one another's faces, and open our hearts to one another in the truth of God once a year, as formerly it used to be. [1668]*[2]

This early general meeting likely was quite large, as are all country-wide meetings. Still the advice establishes that members should be able to see one another and open their hearts to one another in meeting.

Symbol Space[3]

To help us understand the Quaker's gathering circle as an environment Gendlin provides us with the concept of "symbol space". Symbol space is the human environment that we create with our use of language. We form this space and are formed by it as we live our lives.

Symbol space embeds an earlier space called "behavior space" that we share with other animals. In behavior space we likely needed to be physically present to interact.[4] Symbol space is composed of interaction contexts, which we commonly call situations.[5] While we are physically present for most of our interactions, we can engage purely symbolically in some interactions. We can use voting by absentee ballot as an example of a symbolic act. The power of a "symbolic act" lies in the fact that we do not have to be physically present (in space or time) to make changes to our life situation.[6] Still our language and actions are bodily felt. In this sense, symbol space is a *doubled* space, where the patterns of our interactions

---

[2] Britain Yearly Meeting of the Religious Society of Friends, *Quaker Faith & Practice*, 4th edition, 1995-2008, 6.02.

[3] Space means environment. The concept of symbol space is laid out in *APM*, pp. 115-197.

[4] See *APM*, pp. 94-105. In some special instances human infants may show primate behavior.

[5] *APM*, pp. 150-166.

[6] *APM*, pp. 97-98.

are still bodily felt and bodily sensed.[7] Our living sequences generate and regenerate symbol space.

Moreover, our interactions in situations are not lost. What we call *language* and *culture* form in each interaction. Notice we engage in only one interaction. Language and culture are not formed separately.[8] Culture is the collected interaction contexts that we bodily sense, and language is the collected use of words in those interaction contexts. Our knowing how to use any word comes to us as a crossing of the collected interaction contexts (uses of the word) and our present situation, our present using of the word. Our "knowing" how to use a word in a situation comes to us in our implying in a situation, our implying of the change we "need" in the situation.

If we now look more closely at the language that Quakers use to describe their practice in silent meeting, we can understand the interaction contexts (situations) that commonly occur in meeting. Here are a few Quaker words and phrases: "kindling", "centering down", "opening", "leading", "way will open", "sense of the meeting", "minuting", "seasoning", "rise from meeting", and "speak truth to power". These words and phrases help mark off Quaker culture from the larger cultures surrounding silent meetings.

Two Starting Points

Gendlin provides us with two starting points in further understanding the implicit process inherent in the Quaker meeting. These are how we greet a friend, and how we express ourselves:

Greeting a Friend[9]

Let's examine what happens when you greet a close friend. Say you have a friend, Julie, and you happen to come upon Julie on the street. You instantly "know" how tall Julie is, what she looks like, and what her mood is by her body looks and facial expression. You "know" all the ups and downs of your past relationship. You have a feeling sense of Julie. Your feeling sense is not one of individual bits of information. Rather your feeling sense comes as "all about Julie", and it comes "all at once". "All about

---

[7] Interaction patterns are doubled in the sense that behavior space is embedded in symbol space.
[8] If we wish, we can view them separately. See *APM,* pp. 180-185.
[9] *APM*, pp. 51-57.

ulie" also includes how you might talk to her, what tone of voice you may use, and what gestures you may use when you greet her. All of that past is crossed with your present sense of Julie. "All about Julie" shapes how you greet her. And you make your greeting explicit. "Hi, Julie... " Your speaking (and your gestures) is the occurring (next step) into the implying of how you greet Julie in that situation.[10]

When we greet someone we already have a feeling sense of the other person in our implying in the situation. *The other person is always already present in our implying in the situation.* When we are sitting in meeting we already have a feeling sense of others seated in the meeting, and of others as they enter to take their places in the meeting's circle, and we have a feeling sense of the meeting as a whole. All of those feeling senses are crossed in our implying as we seek our (occurring) next step to settle into meeting.

Expression

When we express ourselves, we interact with our environment[11]. When we express ourselves in meeting we are interacting with and within our gathering circle. In symbol space our gathering circle is the situation, the interaction context, and includes all those present.

Expressing is occurring into implying. In expressing we speak from and into our implying to another in a situation. When we express our self to another person, that person is *always already present* in our implying in the situation.[12] What each of us expresses in an interaction is already affected by the other. As you speak you imply some response. When we receive a response that carries us forward, we continue by speaking further in the situation. We carry forward when our speaking satisfies our implying, changing it into a new implying.

When we express ourselves, we experience a series of bodily "feeling" changes in the situation as we carry forward.[13] This series of "feeling"

---

[10] *APM*, pp. 46-47. Gendlin uses the term focaling for this "many into one" aspect in our experiencing of implying. Again, he makes up a word because there are no words with the intended meaning.

[11] *PM*, pp. 17-19.

[12] *APM*, pp. 30-35. Here we are looking at dialogue, but the concept is the same for speaking to a group.

[13] Gendlin calls expression a re-cognition. See *APM*, pp. 218-219.

changes is our perception of our speaking *and* the other person's response to our speaking. In process terms when we express ourselves in a situation, we speak *from* and *into* our on-going implying of the situation. When we express ourselves, we form a series of focal, relevant words or phrases. We are carried forward by our own speaking *and* by another's response to our speaking. In this sense, our expressing is both *reflexive* (bent back) as we hear ourselves speak, and *reflective* from another's response. Reflective means the other person reflects our speaking in some form. The first form of reflection (response) is empathy.[14]

Now, we may consider in this instance why the Quakers advise sitting in a circle to see one another's faces. When a member rises to speak, it helps that member when he or she senses that other members turn their attention to the speaker. Further, the speaker may receive some reflection to his or her speaking. The reflection often is a quite subtle sense of empathy, or simply the posture of a close friend showing that she is deeply listening to the speaker. A reflection showing some empathy or a sense of affirmation will help the speaker carry forward. Further, Quakers advise speaking of a concern or issue that will carry to all the members present. The intent is to avoid a back and forth exchange between members. Such an exchange can impede the flow of the meeting and fail to carry the whole of the meeting forward.

Unfolding A Silent Meeting

Previously we had mentioned the importance Quakers place on preparing the meeting for worship by having some members arrive early and enter into a deep and accepting silence.

Preparation

As we have seen in both the examples of greeting and expression, when we enter into meeting we already have a feeling sense of others in our implying, both those already seated and those also entering. If a meeting is to carry forward in silence and in speaking, then it needs to settle, or in Quaker terms, the members need to "center down". This work of the early helping members, who have a feeling sense of those who are distracted when they enter, is to help their fellow members settle into the silence.

---

[14] *APM*, pp. 119-120.

Thomas Kelly calls these preparations, "kindling":

> One condition for... a group experience seems to be this: some individuals need already, upon entering the meeting, to be gathered deep in the spirit of worship. There must be some kindled hearts when the meeting begins. In them, and from them, begins the work of worship. The spiritual devotion of a few persons, silently deep in active adoration, is needed to kindle the rest, to help those who enter the service with tangled, harried, distraught thoughts to be melted, quieted and released and made pliant, ready for the work of God... [15]

Silence

For those who have attended a Quaker meeting the silence in meeting is palpably different after the first fifteen or twenty minutes. The silence offers a sense of flow. Sometimes meetings extend the silence throughout the worship hour. Such meetings are not common, but they are not rare.

Since words are not spoken, we have only the barest of recollections from such meetings to consider. Again here is Thomas Kelly:

> Certainly the deepness of the covering of a meeting is not proportional to the number of words spoken. A gathered meeting may proceed entirely in silence, rolling with increasing depth and intensity until the meeting breaks and tears are furtively brushed away. Such really powerful hours of unbroken silence frequently carry a genuine progression of spiritual change and experience. These are filled moments... Outwardly, all silences seem alike... But inwardly... the silence bring[s] an inward climax which is definitive as the climax of the mass, when the host is elevated in adoration.[16]

If we consider that the meeting members were engaged in light-type med-

---

[15] Thomas Kelly, *The Gathered Meeting*, p. 13. Also see Tom Gates, *Worship "The Gathered Meeting" Revisited*, Philadelphia Yearly Meeting, 2006, pp. 6-13 for a discussion of conditions that favor a gathered meeting.

[16] Thomas Kelly, p.15.

itations, holding their situations and letting implying come as it may, then we may conclude that the members touched an inward implicit space, and experienced a felt shift that carried their lives forward. We infer that Kelly's climax reflects a felt shift among the members and the meeting as a whole.

Speaking

While a meeting may proceed without members speaking, most meetings experience members rising and speaking. Again, those rising to speak, speak from a leading. They have a feeling sense for others and the meeting as a whole in their implying as they speak; and the members who are listening have a feeling sense of the speaker in their implying as they enter into the occurring (act) of listening.

How the meeting flows depends on how the speaking *interaffects* the members. If the speaking resonates with those listening, then a feeling sense of movement flows among the members. The silence between speakers acts as a bridge rather than a barrier. Quakers value plain speaking. Such speaking often is humble, brief, and sincere and does not contain rhetorical flourishes. When two or three speakers continue with a theme, their speaking may carry the meeting to a climax until the meeting is ended.[17]

Since meeting members do not keep notes, we cannot say how a meeting flows or is checked when resistance comes into play. One rare anecdote from Thomas Kelly offers some insight into how members may interconnect and *interaffect* one another. He recounts the following inward joining:

> *John Hughes once told of two Friends sitting side by side in ... a gathered meeting. The secret currents of worship flowed with power and encountered a check. One man moved nervously but did not rise to his feet. Finally the other Friend arose and spoke a few words of searching power, and the meeting proceeded in a sense of covering. After the meeting had broken the man who had spoken nudged his silent neighbor and said 'Next time, Henry, say it thyself'.*[18]

---

[17] The development of a theme by speakers in a meeting often is referred to as the "exercise of the meeting". For a fuller description of developing the vocal ministry in meeting, see Tom Gates, *Worship "The Gathered Meeting Revisited,* 2006.

[18] Tom Gates, p. 6.

Unity

When Quakers come together openly and honestly share with one another, they experience a sense of unity. They know that they belong together. They trust one another, and they can do together what they cannot do apart. In a gathered meeting, they experience a felt sense of unity as their crossings in their implying *interaffect* one another. Again if we turn to George Fox, we find:

> *All we that are in the light are in unity; for the light is but one...*
> *George Fox [1654]*[19]

As the light symbolizes implying, Quakers experience a deep sense of *unity as they experience their implying as one implying*. They experience a felt shift as they are carried forward, and as the whole meeting is carried forward in a "climax".[20]

Quakers recognize that meetings commonly do not flow to a "climax". More often than not, they encounter a check, or a series of checks as speakers may change the course of speaking by raising different concerns, or some may lack depth in their speaking. Equally likely some members may hold back and not fully share in the meeting, failing to rise to speak or by withdrawing, unable to sustain their listening. When a meeting is checked in some form, members still come away with some sense of fulfillment by having shared an hour together. Often they express a sense of "fellowship". Still, once experienced there also is always a seeking after "unity".

Measures and Weighty Friends

The long-term sustainability of Quaker meetings stems in large measure from how members treat one another and how they welcome new attenders. Treating each other openly and honestly leads to a deep sharing. The early Quaker term for how a member might contribute spiritually to a meeting is "measure". Friends recognized that each member has a limited spiritual understanding, a limited "measure", and that they need one another to share their insights. Here is advice from *Quaker Faith & Practice*:

---

[19] Modern translation by Rex Ambler, *TotH*, 2:18
[20] The Quaker experience pointing to one implying is a step beyond Gendlin's *APM*. It does not contradict Gendlin's *APM*, but is not found in Gendlin's *APM*.

> *Are there not different states, different degrees, different growth, different places?... Therefore, watch every one to feel and know his own place, and service to the body, and to be sensible of the gifts, places, and services of others, that the Lord may be honoured in all, and every one owned and honoured in the Lord, and not otherwise. Isaac Pennington [1667]*[21]

Quakers recognize that all members and attenders have different skills and value to contribute to a meeting, and that every "spiritual" contribution will not be the same. The Quaker practice is to look for and value each person's contribution to meeting. Members treat one another with equality and honesty, affirming and respecting who they are and what they contribute to meeting. This means they value the contribution of the person who gets the mail, or looks after the library as much as they value the person who clerks the meeting.

In earlier times many meetings blessed and recognized those with spiritual gifts as ministers among Friends. In our more modern times, meetings recognize persons within the meeting who have gifts in "spiritual discernment". These persons often clerk meetings, sit on committees, or have a gift for speaking in meeting. These persons are informally recognized within the meeting as "weighty Friends". The term arises from Friends giving more "weight" to what such a Friend may think or say on an issue of concern to members, or to the meeting. Meetings often look to these Friends for leadership.

The Nayler Effect

Like any social process the Quaker meeting is subject to the downside of conflicts that arise within a meeting, or in the larger Society of Friends. Perhaps, the greatest danger occurs when a leading Quaker acts in a way that damages a meeting, or Quaker standing in society.

The early Quakers experienced just such a devastating effect with the arrest, imprisonment, and punishment of James Nayler. In 1656, Nayler was a prominent Quaker minister, whose followings often approached George Fox's in size. His leading at the time was to preach about the rampant "social injustices" in England. However, he failed to restrain his followers,

---

[21] Britain Yearly Meeting, *Quaker Faith & Practice*, 4th Edition, 1995-2008, 10:27.

whose behaviors outraged the authorities and the church. The London Yearly Meeting provides the following account:

> *In 1655, Nayler came south to help work in London, where he became ensnared by flatterers, who behaved themselves in an extravagant fashion, bowing, kneeling and singing before him. On going to Bristol he was persuaded by Friends there to see Fox then in Launceston jail, but on the way he was taken and imprisoned at Exeter. He was freed in October 1656, and a few days later entered Bristol on horseback with his followers around him. They spread garments before him and sang, "Holy, Holy, Lord God of Israel". The authorities interfered and sent him to London, where Parliament after long debates sentenced him to imprisonment after being whipped and pilloried in London and Bristol, and branded for a blasphemer, and having his tongue bored through.*[22]

The fall of Nayler came just 4 years after Fox came to the North of England in 1652. Following Nayler's arrest and imprisonment, the nascent Quaker movement was subject to increasing rounds of imprisonment. The gravity of the situation is emphasized by the fact that Nayler's punishment was decided by a trial in Parliament, which was in itself controversial since Parliament is a legislative, not a judicial body. The authorities took Nayler's preaching on social injustices as a call for political revolution. Nayler's case showed the Quaker community's vulnerability to an individual's excessive actions.

George Fox and other Quaker elders responded to the fall out effects of Nayler's arrest and imprisonment. They did so in two ways. First, they began by changing the Quaker's meeting structure. Prior to Nayler, meetings met irregularly and were in loose contact with one another. Fox changed that by urging regular monthly meetings so that meetings could identify and resolve conflicts with those they called "disorderly walkers", and look

---

[22] Quoted in Michael Sheeran, *Beyond Majority Rule*, Philadelphia Yearly Meeting, 1996, p. 9. This is an overly harsh view of Nayler. Nayler's ride into Bristol was intended as a re-enactment of Christ's entry into Jerusalem. A more modern view is that Nayler was severely depressed and not in a position to restrain his followers. See: http://bcw-ptoject.org/biography/james-nayler.

after those members who were imprisoned. Second, Fox put in place the means to distill advice for meetings by and from larger gatherings, General Meetings of ministers and elders. These larger gatherings evolved into what we now know as yearly meetings. These yearly meetings have taken on the task of publishing "Advices and Queries" for their member monthly meetings. One early set of advices came in 1656 from a General Meeting of the Elders of Balby with the following advice for addressing members "who walked disorderly", or flouted common standards of behavior:

> *Persons who walk disorderly are to be spoken to in private, then before two or three witnesses; then, if necessary, the matter is to be reported to the Church. The Church is to reprove them for their disorderly walking, and, if they do not reform, the case is to be sent in writing to 'some whom the Lord hath raised up in the power of the spirit of the Lord to be fathers, -- His children to gather in the light' so that the thing may be known to the body and be determined in the light.*[23]

The statement sets out a discipline by a monthly meeting with discipline by Quaker leaders as a last resort. The following postscript by the Elders of Balby (below) makes clear that their prescriptions for resolving conflict are advice – not rules. Each meeting should face and resolve their conflicts by getting at the "truth of the matter". Holding one another in the "light" and letting the truth come in and through the meeting as a whole, can and does lead to a resolution of conflict. Resolutions found in this way tend to endure. Here is the Elder's postscript:

> *Dearly beloved Friends, these things we do not lay upon you as a rule or form to walk by, but that all, with the measure of light which is pure and holy, may be guided: and so in the light walking and abiding, these may be fulfilled in the Spirit, not from the letter, for the letter killeth, but the Spirit giveth life. Elders of Balby [1656]*[24]

---

[23] Quoted in Friends General Conference, *The Wounded Meeting,* Friends General Conference, 1993. p. 7.
[24] Quoted in Michael Sheeran, *Beyond Majority Rule*, p. 13.

Rather than set rules, George Fox and the Elders choose to resolve conflicts by advising a process of "reconciliation". Their basic advice to monthly meetings has persisted. Distilled in a modern form the Quaker advice is that when meetings take corrective measures to resolve conflict: (1) The measures should grow out of love, not anger; (2) the measures should result from a meeting's discernment; (3) offenders should be spoken to in private with only a few members present; and (4) public censure should occur only as a last resort.[25]

The recommended form for the initial private contact with the offending person is that it comes from a regular meeting committee, like the Ministry or Oversight Committee, or a Special Committee formed for the purpose of meeting with the person. Public censure should only occur as a last resort when the matter has been moved before the whole meeting.

The Wounded Meeting

While the general advice on handling conflicts is helpful, meetings still must develop responses to deal with disruptions. The modern Quaker meeting is especially vulnerable as meeting membership declines and the experience and resources within the meeting may be stretched to deal with disruptions to the meeting for worship.

In the early 1990's The Friends General Conference in Philadelphia formed a task group to develop information from meetings about the types of disruptions that they were encountering and giving examples of meeting responses. Their findings were published in a small booklet called, *The Wounded Meeting*.[26]

The Task Group divided situations into three types: (1) situations most easily addressed; (2) more difficult situations; and (3) exceptionally difficult situations.

Situations Most Easily Addressed

Those situations that were easily addressed arose from an "unawareness, mis-understanding, or forgetfulness" about Quaker practices, especially the need for silence and careful thought before speaking in meeting. We have talked about this issue in the context of meetings that often

---

[25] Friends General Conference, *The Wounded Meeting*, p. 8.
[26] Friends General Conference, pp. 3-32.

attract many visitors unfamiliar with Quakers ways. Meetings faced with this type of disruption responded by putting out placards describing the meeting for worship and what was expected of members and attenders. The following is a placard used by a meeting in Washington, DC:

> *[The Meeting] welcomes you to meeting for worship. Our meeting for worship is a silent, unprogrammed worship service. A period of time, perhaps twenty minutes, is needed to center down into the inward stillness of Quaker worship. Our spoken messages come from the spiritual depth of one's life and from the leading of the Holy Spirit. To be absorbed, each message needs to be followed with a period of silence. When a message speaks to the condition of those present and is harmoniously developed and deepened, a profound sense of spiritual community may occur among us that freshens and delights. This is what we call a 'gathered meeting'. Meeting for worship ends after about an hour...* [27]

In many cases simply handing out the placard was sufficient to alleviate the disruptions. Alternatively, some meetings assigned members to meet with and talk with new attenders following the meeting for worship, sharing the placard and answering any questions that the person might have about Quaker worship.

More Difficult Situations

Meetings faced with long-standing disruptive behaviors face a more difficult situation. Generally meetings are willing to bear with short-term behaviors, like overlong or loud, unhelpful speaking if the person does not persist, or if he or she attends for only a short period of time. Persistent disruptive behavior varies from case to case. The meeting is left to sort out and attempt to address the behavior. Often as the task group suggests, the behavior arises from an unmet need of the person involved.

I can think of one case in my home meeting that falls into this category. This situation concerned a member, whom we shall call Karl. Karl had a problem drinking and was in a dreadful car accident. Following the

---

[27] Friends General Conference, p.10.

accident he underwent brain surgery. The surgery left him disfigured and partially impaired his thinking and speaking. Karl was divorced from his wife Sonia. They had two children, a boy, who was about 7 and a daughter who was 5. Karl's wife Sonia attended meeting and the children were regular attenders in the First Day (Sunday) School.

After he recovered from his surgery Karl sought to attend meeting. However, he often was drunk and we turned him away. When he was sober he rose to speak in meeting. His speaking was emotional, disjointed and hard to understand, but was usually focused on his children and his thankfulness to the meeting for looking after his children in First Day School. While he was enjoined from visiting his children or having them visit him, he could and did see his children briefly after meeting.

Our meeting under the guidance of the Ministry and First Day School Committees met to discuss how we might work with Karl to temper his emotional outbursts in meeting. Clearly we could see that Karl was drawn to meeting because of his children. His need palpably was to see his children. We worked out a plan for an informal group of three or four members from the meeting to meet with Karl when he came to meeting. If he was drunk, we escorted him to a small building on the meeting grounds and talked to him, calming him down before escorting him away. If he was sober, one of us would accompany him into meeting and stay with him during and after meeting when he met briefly with his children. His ex-wife Sonia supported the meeting's efforts to work with Karl. It made her life easier. She had to spend less time and effort fending of his phone calls and attempts to visit his children.

After Karl's situation was semi-stable, the meeting with the support of Sonia worked out an arrangement with Social Services where Karl could visit his children after First Day School on a pre-arranged basis. The visits were to take place on the meeting grounds, and one or two meeting members were to be present to oversee the visits. Expressed in Quaker terms the visits were "under the care of the meeting". This arrangement worked well for a few years. Karl came to meeting sober. He tempered his speaking. He became a regular attender, mostly unnoticed by those who were unfamiliar with his history. This situation lasted until Sonia moved out of state and took the children with her. After her move Karl drifted away from the meeting.

Karl's case shows the time, energy and effort that a meeting may need to extend to resolve difficult cases of disruption. However, our meeting like others working through difficult situations found our efforts deeply gratifying as our meeting carried forward.

Exceptionally Difficult Situations

The Friends' Task Group found several cases where meetings were disrupted by difficult behaviors, and where the meetings were unable to reach the disruptors in any meaningful way. Many of these disruptors exhibited bizarre behaviors. One woman, for example, would read papers and magazines during meeting, talking loudly as she did in a running commentary on what she was reading. She also would go to the piano and loudly play and sing hymns. Unable to reason with the woman in private meetings, the meeting eventually barred the woman from attending meeting for worship.

In most of these exceptionally difficult situations, the individual meetings were taxed beyond their resources and had to ask for outside help. Help now is available from quarterly and yearly meetings, where skilled counselors may come and help a meeting members work through their situation. In many cases meetings simply had to seek court orders to keep the disruptive person from attending meeting. Often meetings struggled in their responses, in some cases for years before finally disowning the attender and getting a court order to keep him or her away. In the Task Group's view meetings often waited too long to arrive at that decision, losing members and attenders as people dropped out of the meeting. Some meetings were severely wounded in the process and jeopardized their long-term viability.

Other Difficult Situations – Split Between God-Centered and Universalist Friends

One area troubling many meetings that the Task Group did not address is the differences that may arise between God-centered Friends and Universalist (Progressive) Friends attending meeting. Rather than the break in meetings that occurs in situations addressed by the Task Force, the differences in religious preferences among Friends in a meeting may produce something more like a long-term debilitating condition. This God-centered split comes from a generations-long ambivalence and unwillingness of many Friends to reconcile their expression of faith with the early Friends expressions of faith in Christ.

In my own limited experience with a meeting that experienced a split between Christ-centered members and more Universalist members, I recall that the differences persisted for some time in vocal ministry in the meeting.[28] Our meeting was a small meeting with a Christ-centered family and two or three other like-minded members. More Progressive members made up a majority of members. Eventually the split surfaced over what lessons the meeting should teach in the First Day School. The meeting was unable to resolve the lesson issue. Soon after the Christ-centered family and at least one other member left the meeting.

Michael Sheeran looked at the question of this type of religious split more closely while observing and interviewing members of meetings in the Philadelphia Yearly Meeting.[29] Sheeran concluded that the cleavage between Christ-centered and Universalist-type members offered too simplistic view of what was happening in meetings. Rather, he found that a more fundamental split existed between those meetings that had experienced a gathered meeting and those that had not. He reported:

> *[I] began to find that Christocentric and certain universalists shared a sort of profound reverence for the gathered meeting for worship which was not found among other Friends… Their words to explain the experience varied markedly, of course, but for both groups, the experience itself is what counted… Put simply, the real cleavage among Friends is between those who experience the gathered or covered condition and those who do not… the words and concepts are secondary; the event, the experience is what counts.*[30]

In other words, if a meeting can and does gather, then that meeting can accommodate multiple religious views. In my own reporting (above), the meeting that I observed was unable to gather, and eventually split.

An Implicit Process Underlying Social Change

What can we learn about the implicit process underlying the Quaker responses to wounded meetings?

---

[28] Sadly, this was my home meeting in Reno, NV.
[29] Michael Sheeran, *Beyond Majority Rule*, p.5.
[30] Tom Gates, *Worship "The Gathered Meeting" Revisited*, p. 5. Quoting Michael Sheeran, *Beyond Majority Rule*, p. 5. Italics added.

So far, we have looked at the implicit process that unfolds in the Quaker meeting for worship where the focus is on members "holding and letting" the "truth" come to them.

If we take a step back, we can look at the meeting itself. Using the Quaker phrase we can look at "the life of the meeting." A meeting is not static; it is constantly regenerating. Members move away or die. New members and attenders join the meeting. Committee clerks change. Each time the meeting gathers in a circle for worship that is a new gathering. The implying that carries the life of the meeting forward is an intricate crossing of known and as yet unknown needs.

Stoppage

Here let us introduce a new implicit process term: *stoppage*.[31] Stoppage occurs when an occurring does not change an implying as implying implies itself changed. In this sense implying cannot carry forward in the same way. All occurring is into implying, even in a stoppage. We then may go on differently, now missing what was stopped. Or, alternatively a novel changed occurring may carry our implying forward in a new way.

If we turn to the life of the meeting, we can say it is analogous to our own living body. We constantly regenerate our body as cells die and are replaced. When we suffer a wound, our implying is stopped, our on-going implying carries that stopped process. We cannot fully carry our life forward until our wound is healed and our implying is carried forward again in a new way. The healing may come from our own internal body healing processes, or it may come when we seek outside help with sutures and antibiotics. Our carrying forward is different; it now includes the experience of our wound stoppage and recovery.

> *When we experience a stoppage as a check in the flow of our living forward, we recognize a stoppage as what falls out of our implying.[32] When we come to recognize a stoppage, we say "Oh! That's the problem."*

The Quaker's wounded meetings offer an apt description of stoppage in the underlying implicit process that carries the life of the meeting for-

---

[31] *APM*, pp. 20-32.
[32] A stoppage occurs. It may or may not be recognized.

ward. In my own meeting's case where we started working with Karl's disruptions to our meeting for worship, our meeting was *stuck* the first few times Karl attended. There was little or no flow to the meeting.

The first step in healing our meeting was to meet with Karl when he came to meeting to see if he was sober, and sit with him during meeting. This first step of working with Karl was a slow process. Gradually we found we could temper Karl's speaking in meeting. Part of the process was Karl getting to know us and was enhanced by the fact that we also looked after his children in First Day School.

The second major step was getting Social Services to agree to have the meeting oversee Karl's visits with his children. One person in our volunteer group was familiar with the workings of Social Services. When we were informally sitting together she suggested we contact the children's mother Sonia to see if she would agree to have the meeting oversee Karl's visits with his children. If so, then we would contact Social Services. Sonia agreed and we took our leading to the Ministry Committee. The committee agreed with us and put the concern to the whole meeting at the next monthly business meeting. After some consideration the meeting wrote a minute approving a proposal to Social Services, setting out the limits of what the meeting would offer: a pre-arranged visit with one or two meeting members present, confined to the meeting grounds or the adjacent public playground and limited to two hours.

While unusual, Social Services eventually approved the meeting's visit proposal with Sonia's consent. At first Karl tried to test the limits of the agreement by asking to see the children longer, or asking to take them elsewhere. However, we were firm in sticking to agreement. The meeting absorbed Karl as a semi-regular member in meeting for worship, and as I reported (above) the arrangement worked well for a few years until Sonia moved out of state with the children.

By testing our volunteer leadings to have Karl's visits with his children take place under the "care of the meeting", the whole of the meeting came to understand and approve of our working with Karl. At the business meeting several members helped in drafting the minute for the proposal to Social Services so that it was clear and concise in setting out what the meeting would do. The meeting was no longer *stuck* with Karl. We felt our leadings in working with Karl deepened the "life of the meeting". After a partial stoppage with Karl, our wounded meeting healed and the life of our meeting carried forward in a different way, enriched by our working through the stoppage together.

Revisiting the Nayler Effect

Unlike the stoppages that Quakers encounter in individual meetings, the Nayler crisis produced a stoppage in the whole nascent Quaker movement. George Fox's and the elder's responses were immediate – and creative. We can assume that their responses came from "holding and letting", waiting for the next steps, the "truth". While the idea of setting out an advice of reconciliation with "disorderly walkers" and not setting hard and fast rules was in keeping with the early Quaker practices, the structural changes that Fox proposed and carried out were new. As we have said, the early Quaker meetings for worship were irregular. Fox called for regular monthly meetings to conduct the business of the meeting, chiefly to deal with the disorderly and provide support for those imprisoned, the "sufferers". The term "monthly meeting" comes from this call for a regular monthly meeting for business. Further, Fox called for and facilitated general meetings. The meeting of the Elders of Balby was one of the first such meetings. The effect of both changes was to shift the early Quaker focus from individual leadings of change and transformation to the monthly meeting where leadings could be (and were) tested, and to the general meetings that distilled and passed on advices on Quaker practices to the monthly meetings. These early general meetings evolved into our modern yearly meetings. The yearly meetings now provide advice in the form of "Advices and Queries" to their monthly member meetings. These Advices and Queries are contained in a book of *Faith and Practice* published periodically by most yearly meetings. Both reforms have endured.

If we consider that Fox's proposed changes came from "holding and letting", then we can see that what we call a "social structure" arises from our on-going implying. This new creative social form comes from the same crossing and interaffecting that we experience in our own lives. Here we have Fox and the elders finding a new way forward for the "lives of the meetings". However, rather than consider this new meeting structure a one-off situation, if we look more closely we see that such structures are a continuous part of our on-going implying. We can use the term *structur-*

ing to describe our on-going implying in social situations.³³ *Structuring* is a continuous process. Our implying is always far more intricate and orderly than we can understand. Structuring is present each time a Quaker circle gathers. Out of these gatherings, when Quakers sit "holding" a concern for the life of the meeting and "letting" the truth come, the structuring of the meetings and the Society as a whole can evolve over time. As we have suggested, the general meetings of the early Quakers evolved into our modern yearly meetings. This social form has endured over time while undergoing continuous change.

Revisiting the Gathered Meeting

In 2006 the Philadelphia Yearly Meeting published a booklet by Tom Gates called *Worship "The Gathered Meeting" Revisited*.³⁴ As the title suggests, Gates revisits Thomas Kelly's essay on *The Gathered Meeting*. Gates was responding to a concern about the continued decline of gathered meetings among Friends. Starting out he cites Michael Sheeran's view that the major division among Friends is not between God-centered Friends and more Universalist (Progressive) Friends, rather it is between those Friends who have experienced a gathered meeting, and those who have not. For example, Sheeran reported on interviews offering both viewpoints:

> *Said one Friend: 'Why make such a big thing out of this gathered meeting business? That's surely not attracted me to Quakerism, and Quakers get along by and large without it'.*
>
> *As if in reply, another longtime Friend remarked: 'We have gotten a lots of new members, especially in recent years, who are attracted by our testimonies – peace, racial harmony, women's rights, and the like. But it seems to me that most of these people will eventually leave us unless they become **turned on by our worship**. If they don't find something very special here, they will become impatient because we aren't so single-minded about such causes as they are. They'll tire of our slowness and they'll leave. After all we try to base our actions on divine leadings,*

---

³³ *APM*, p. 32.
³⁴ Tom Gates, *Worship "The Gathered Meeting" Revisited*, Philadelphia Yearly Meeting, 2006.

> *we're more interested in finding the divine than in any cause taken by itself'.*[35]

Now nearly two decades after Sheeran's work with meetings in the Philadelphia Yearly Meeting, Quaker meetings have become even more complex. In addition to God-centered Friends, Progressive Friends, and social activists, we are likely to have some Friends who practice Mindfulness or some eastern meditative practice. Our more complex meetings have a yet greater need to gather, to heal any rifts that may arise among meeting members. However, the increasing rarity of gathered meetings lessens the likelihood that members will have experienced a gathered meeting. We can think of the many ungathered meetings as having a *partial stoppage*, or alternatively as never having experienced fully carrying forward the life of the meeting.

Expressed in Quaker terms, a gathered experience is a "right ordering" of a meeting. For meetings experiencing rifts among members, a gathered meeting can heal the rifts and divisions among its members. Once experienced the memory of the gathering is not lost among members. It is a profound experience and can last a lifetime. The experience is carried forward in the members' implying of the meeting and in their own lives.

Implicit Space[36]

Why then is a gathered meeting such a profound experience for the members and the meeting as a whole?

Let's return to the gathering circle, the environment that Quakers create with their silent meeting. At its core the meeting practice is to get to a "place beyond words", to an "opening" where change and transformation can occur. Gendlin calls this space that Quakers seek, "Implicit Space", an environment that is beyond words.

> *We experience Implicit space as a doubling in our patterns of living as we interact with our implying. Symbol space is embedded in implicit space.*

---

[35] Michael Sheeran, *Beyond Majority Rule*, pp. 88-89. Quoted in Tom Gates, p. 6. **Sheeran's emphasis.**
[36] The concept of Implicit Space is laid out in *APM* Chapter VIII, pp. 198-241.

One constant constraint in our modern living is that our patterns of interacting (in symbol space), our speaking and acting have become so complex that we rarely experience a deep sense of living forward. Our living is experiencing patterns as just that – patterns – and little more. If you like, we can say that our symbol space is filling up. We need to get beyond our everyday words and actions to again live forward. We do this by interacting with our implying.

One way that we can think further about implicit space is to understand how we think about time. We commonly think about time as linear time. We think of past, present and future as positions on a timeline. Viewing our living as a process yields quite a different view of time. Our first impulse is to think of occurring as the present, and implying as the future, but this is not the case. Occurring into implying carries our own implying forward so that we enact our own living, our own process. With this process model implying is changed if the living process is carried forward, but implying always remains part of the on-going occurring. The past and future are the internal continuity of our body's own process. We experience time as an aspect of our on-going occurring into implying.[37]

In our living as a process there are no fixed time (or space) relationships. Time relationships are regenerated in each occurring event. The "past" (antecedent) possibilities are not fixed. What is relevant is formed in each occurring. We only know the set of possibilities retroactively after the event. The process model leads to a functioning past in the present and a functioning future in the present. *The actual event changes the system of possibilities.* The possibilities, which the event regenerates, may not have been possibilities that entered into the event. Our implying functions as a more intricate future.

Now let us return to a gathered meeting. What occurs as the meeting gathers is that the implying of the meeting and its members' implying becomes one implying. As the members speak from a felt sense forming in that space beyond words, then the whole meeting can carry forward in a way that none could have foreseen. Implying carries a future function of all possible ways forward, and the forming felt sense opens the one relevant way forward for the life of the meeting. Further, the meeting

---

[37] *APM*, pp. 58-70.

experiences a sense of direction and purpose. Our sense of purpose, direction and meaning are part of our living process, from carrying our living forward. Out of the gathering, out of implicit space, an unforeseen living way forward can come to the meeting. This is the felt shift climax of a gathered meeting.[38]

What Can Modern Quaker Meetings Do?

Gates, along with the Friends that he quotes, realizes and states clearly that you cannot seek a gathering directly. You cannot will or plan a gathered meeting. A felt sense for a meeting only forms as it can form. We do not know our relevant need, or our meeting's need until we meet the situation – holding our concern and letting an answer come to us. All possible answers to and for a meeting are crossed in the meeting members' implying, and crossed further with their past experiences to bring a "truth" that can carry a meeting forward.

What you can do is strengthen the conditions in a meeting that increase the likelihood of a gathered meeting.[39] Following Thomas Kelly, Gates sets out conditions in meetings that will, in Kelly's word "favor" a gathered meeting. He carries two of Kelly's main themes forward: (1) *kindling* the meeting, and (2) developing a *theme* in vocal ministry in the meeting. A modern meeting cannot take either condition for granted. In both instances what came easily to meetings in the past must now be done with conscious intentions.

Kindled Hearts

Besides *kindling* the meeting for worship by coming to meeting early and preparing the meeting with a worshipful silence, Gate suggests that members can go further by deepening their daily spiritual life with prayer and meditation. They can join with others in their meeting by participating in spiritual formation programs that may be offered by Yearly Meetings. Members can learn to know other members better by getting together for dinner, or joining together in a meeting's work programs. In effect,

---

[38] The felt shift experienced by Quakers in a gathered meeting goes a step beyond Gendlin's *Process Model*. Gendlin identifies a personal felt shift. He does not preclude a group felt shift.

[39] Tom Gates, pp. 4 ff.

members can better prepare their lives and character for meeting. Again in Kelly's phrase, they can seek to bring "kindled hearts" to meeting.[40]

A Theme in Ministry

Gates makes the point that there are some meeting events like a marriage or a memorial, which have a natural theme that may lead to a gathered meeting. Or, a meeting may gather as it reaches unity on a contentious issue at a monthly meeting for business. Such a natural theme may arise when a meeting rises to meet a challenge on a social issue. As a current example, many meetings in the southwest US have been challenged to provide sanctuary for illegal immigrants from Mexico. After a series of contentious meetings, the Albuquerque Meeting in New Mexico gathered when they reached unity on providing sanctuary for an illegal immigrant. The Meeting provided sanctuary in the meetinghouse for two years until she was able to safely move on.[41]

Following Kelly's call for a theme to enhance a meeting's vocal ministry, Gates suggests that members need to share their experiences in vocal ministry; learning from one another in how to rise to speak; how to sense and respond to a theme that may develop in meeting; and also sharing what went well and where they think they may have erred in their ministry.

A Last Consideration

Both meeting paths that Gates puts forward point to members consciously preparing themselves for meeting, preparing to listen more deeply, and to knowingly prepare to speak should they sense a leading to speak in ministry to the meeting.

As a last consideration, let's consider what members might be asking as they enter the meetinghouse on First Day for worship. Are they asking:

"What can I bring to worship?' Or, are they asking:

"What am I getting out of worship?"

---

[40] "We bring to meeting on First Day our collectedness or scatteredness, and we help or hinder the meeting accordingly." Elizabeth Watson quoted in Tom Gates, p. 8.

[41] Personal communication from Fred Koster.

As the balance in attitudes shifts towards members looking to see what they can expect to get out of meeting, the spiritual life of the meeting lessens and the conditions for gathered meetings are lessened or lost. We get a hollowing out of the life of the meeting.

Next

We shall turn to look at the Quaker meeting for business, the monthly meeting.

5. WRITING A MINUTE

There is a better understanding among non-Quakers of how Friends go about making decisions in their monthly business meetings than an understanding of the meeting for worship itself. Certainly this better understanding comes from the more transparent nature of a meeting making decisions, and to the fact that the Quaker practice has drawn a wider interest because of the effectiveness of their decision process. Quakers themselves describe their decision making as getting "beyond consensus".[1]

At the center of Quaker decision-making is an effort to get a "sense of the meeting" as to how to decide a concern brought before the meeting. After some discussion and when the meeting's Clerk feels that he or she has an initial "sense" of how the meeting is leaning, the Clerk will move to draft a minute expressing the decision, then read it aloud. This draft in turn may prompt further discernment and revisions until the meeting reaches a point of "unity" that all can agree the matter is decided. The Clerk then records the final version of the minute in the meeting's business record. If "unity" is not reached, then the matter is set aside with the understanding that it will be re-visited at some future meeting.

This decision process appears straightforward, but is extremely difficult to replicate when it is taken out of the context of the Quaker meeting and Quaker practice.

Preparation

Like many Quaker practices advice on how to go about making decisions was set out early on. The following is decision-making advice taken from a pamphlet written by Edward Burrough in 1662:

---

[1] Barry Morley, *Beyond Consensus: salvaging the sense of the meeting*, Pendle Hill Publications, 1993.

> *... Being orderly come together, not to spend time with needless, unnecessary and fruitless discourses, but to proceed in the wisdom of God... to hear and consider... not in the way of the world, as a worldly assembly of men, by hot contest, by seeking to out-speak and over-reach one another in discourse, as if it were controversy between party and party of men, or two sides violently striving for dominion, in the way of carrying some worldly interest for self-advantage; not deciding affairs by the greater vote, or the number of men, as the world, who have not the wisdom and power of God... But in the wisdom, love and fellowship of God, in gravity, patience, meekness, in unity and concord, submitting one to another in lowliness of heart, and in the holy spirit of truth and righteousness, all things to be carried on; by hearing and determining every matter coming before you in love, coolness, gentleness and dear unity. I say, as only one party, all for the truth of Christ... to determine of things by mutual accord, in assenting together as the one man in the spirit of truth and equity, and by the authority thereof. Edward Burrough. [1662]*[2]

As you can see from Burrough's words the Quakers were, and are, quite clear that they are taking a markedly different path to making decisions. Their way is "... not in the way of the world..." They want to get to a deeper more sensitive awareness; they want to see the "truth of the matter". The more familiar ways of vote getting do not account for feelings, relationships, and dynamics inherent in the Quaker meeting. This Quaker way is slower, but it yields better decisions over time. In voting, or in consensus decisions, those out-voted often feel at odds with a decision, others may regret their compromises in reaching a consensus.

Barry Morley makes a clear distinction between consensus and the Quaker way. Consensus comes though:

> *... a process of reasoning in which people search for a satisfactory decision... Through consensus we decide it; through a*

---

[2] Quoted in Rex Ambler, *TQW*, pp. 65-66

sense of the meeting we turn it over, allowing it to be decided. 'Reaching a consensus is a secular process', says a Friend. 'In a sense of the meeting, God gets a voice.'[3]

We have the same familiar process of the Quaker meeting, of members "holding and letting", waiting for an answer, a next step to come from their implying. This "sense of the meeting" comes *through* not from the members, and members come to trust the process as decisions are tested over time.

What makes this decision process possible? Many outsiders looking at this Quaker process fail to understand how it arises from the meeting itself. Members bring the same attitude and openness that they bring to a meeting for worship. In fact the Friend's official title for a business meeting is: "A Meeting for Worship with Attention to Business", or in the UK "Meeting for Worship for Business".

Many meetings hold their monthly business meeting in the afternoon after a meeting for worship in the morning. As in the morning meeting a few members will come early and begin the process of settling the silence, "kindling" the meeting in Kelly's phrase. As others follow, the meeting will take 15 or 20 minutes to "center down" before the clerk sets out the agenda.

The same discipline that guides the morning meeting makes the afternoon meeting for business practicable. The standing advice is to prepare minds not opinions. Members are asked to pause in silence between contributions, to listen attentively, to speak to the meeting as a whole, to speak briefly and to the point, and to avoid speaking in a way that attempts to manipulate others. Further, since the meeting is under the guidance of the Clerk, members are asked to defer to the Clerk and to keep silent while the clerk writes a minute. Finally members are asked to unite on the minute – not on a vote. If the meeting cannot unite on the minute, then members are asked to defer ("season") the issue to another meeting.

The Meeting Clerk's Role

Unlike the meeting for worship, the meeting's clerk plays a significant role in how the monthly meeting for business moves forward. Michael Sheeran, a Jesuit scholar, studied Quaker decision-making in the 1960's by

---

[3] Barry Morley, *Beyond Consensus*, p. 5.

spending two years observing Quaker meetings belonging to the Philadelphia Yearly Meeting. As an outsider he made a particularly astute study of the clerk's role in business meeting. The major points that follow lay along the lines given by Sheeran in his book.[4]

First, Sheeran lays out what makes an effective meeting clerk. He quotes Douglas Steere, a Quaker writer:

> *He or she is a good listener, has a clear mind that can handle issues, has the gift of preparing a written minute that can succinctly sum up the sense of the meeting, and is one who has faith in the presuppositions: ... faith in the presence of a Guide; faith in the deep revelatory genius of such a meeting to arrive at a decision that may break new ground and may in fresh ways be in keeping with the Society of Friends' deepest testimonies; and faith in each of those present being potentially the vehicle of the fresh resolving insight. With all of this, a good clerk is a person who refuses to be hurried and can weary out dissension with a patience borne of the confidence that there is a way through, although the group may have to return again and again to the issue before clearness comes and a proper decision is reached.[5]*

The clerk has several major responsibilities.

Agenda

The Clerk's first responsibility is setting the agenda for the meeting. To do this, she or he must summarize and frame the questions for the various concerns that have been brought forward for the meeting. How the Clerk orders the agenda will have a major effect on how the meeting moves through the agenda. Most Clerks, for example, will put some simple items forward on the agenda so that the meeting can gain some sense of movement before tackling a major concern that may take some time.

---

[4] Michael Sheeran, *Beyond Majority Rule*, pp. 91-106. Sheeran initially was interested in the Quakers because the Jesuit Order at the time of its founding in 1540 had a similar communal decision process that was abandoned after about 100 years. He still has an interest in what he calls "communal discernment."

[5] Michael Sheeran, p. 91.

Unlike the meeting for worship the business meeting usually has no fixed time limit. Still most meetings encounter some time pressures to complete their agenda, especially when they are seeking unity on a difficult issue. Such issues normally come from one of the meeting's committees, the Committee on Ministry, or the Oversight Committee. In these cases, the Clerk may informally sit in on the committee's meeting where the issue is discussed to gain a better understanding of the issue. It is essential for the Clerk to maintain a sense of general neutrality in framing the question for the agenda and the ensuing discussion at the business meeting.

Diplomacy and Discipline

The Clerk has to have a good sense of both diplomacy and discipline to help the meeting work through an agenda and any difficult issues that may reside in the agenda. A major part of his or her task is discerning "who knows what" about an issue, as well as having a sense of those who have chosen not to speak. Indeed, in many cases the task of the Clerk is to seek comments from silent members when he or she senses that they may have a leading to provide clarity on an issue. Often these members constitute a majority in a business meeting. Some Clerks solicit comments from these Friends, recognizing that some members are shy, but may have relevant comments on an issue. Soliciting comments may build support for an issue, or alternatively such comments may draw out a hidden opposition to an issue.

Many Clerks encounter long-winded speakers. It is up to the Clerk to keep these speakers in check so that the meeting may proceed. In the UK a Clerk or an Elder often stands when she or he considers the speaker has gone on long enough.[6] If the speaker persists, another member may rise and point out to the speaker that "the Clerk is standing". This standing practice seems to work well as a discipline and some US meetings have adopted it as a practice as well. Clerks also may encounter "chronic objectors". A clerk may disregard objections from such members, or record an objection in the minute and move on. Clerks develop their own styles in dealing with these types of objections. Sheeran comments that a "gracious, but firm" response is a common element in effective styles of clerking.

---

[6] UK Meetings maintain a strong tradition of Elders and they play or a more active role in both meeting for worship and meeting for business.

Reading the Sense of the Meeting

Far and away, the Clerk's most important responsibility is "reading" the sense of the meeting. Such reading entails making judgments about whether a proposal is a valid sense of the meeting, or whether the weight of the meeting is divided. The clerk needs to sense whether a proposal is trending in a favorable way. If that is the case, then he or she may offer a proposed minute to further the discernment. Alternatively, if the Clerk senses that there is no trend, then he or she will usually delay offering a minute.

These sense of the meeting judgments often are difficult and not at all obvious. As an example Sheeran recounts how a gathered condition arose at a business meeting of the American Friends Service Committee (AFSC). An AFSC staff member gave an account of the AFSC meeting on deciding to care for refugees in Gaza:

> *In 1948, there were 750,000 refugees on the Gaza Strip; the new state of Israel had just been established. The UN asked AFSC to take responsibility for feeding, housing, etc. At the meeting of the AFSC Board of Directors, all speakers said the work needed doing, but all agreed it was just too big for the Service Committee. They counseled that we should say no, with regrets. Then the chairman called for a period of silence, prayer, and meditation. Ten or fifteen minutes went by in which no one spoke. The chairman opened the discussion once again. The view around the table completely changed: 'Of course, we have to do it.' There was complete unity.*[7]

How did the Chairman (clerking the meeting) read that the sense of the meeting was counter to all the discussion that had gone on? Obviously he had some sense of a deeper unity in the meeting when he called for silence and some reflection.

The ability to read the sense of the meeting does not rest solely with the Clerk. Other experienced members often may help. Again Sheeran talked with an experienced Friend just after the conclusion of a business meeting where the Friend rose to speak at a critical juncture on an issue

---

[7] Michael Sheeran, p.83.

before the meeting. His speaking brought the meeting to unity. Sheeran remarks on what he learned:

> Here, then, is a combination of ability to read the community's attitudes and to lead the community to a new unity. The speaker is doing two things at once. The two cannot be separated. Because he knows the extent of their unity of desire, he is able to call them to a unity of commitment to a course of action. The latter unity does not exist before he calls them. This ability to judge not only the unity that is real but also the unity that is now possible is in the deepest sense the charisma, which marks Quaker leadership.[8]

Leadership Issues

With so much authority vested in the Clerk to lead the business meeting, there is an obvious danger for Clerks to abuse their authority and manipulate outcomes. Sheeran suggests such abuses are quite rare. Meeting Clerks show remarkable self-restraint and uniformly view their clerking as a deeply felt reverential service to their meeting. Further, as Sheeran found in talking to one Clerk, the meeting can (and often does) act as a check on a Clerk:

> There's no way to make sure the clerk does everything perfectly. The behavior of the members can readily act as a control on the clerk, however. If someone of some significance mentions from the floor that he doubts the minute was correct, the clerk may have reason to take this as a warning shot across the bow! If things are wandering, someone from the floor can encourage the clerk to give direction by asking the clerk to suggest a minute. Today that happened to me. At the meeting just concluded, others' questions obliged me as clerk to offer tentative minutes.[9]

One leadership issue that is more likely to affect the meeting's behavior is a clear and persistent deference to the Clerk by many meeting

---

[8] Michael Sheeran p. 103.
[9] Michael Sheeran, p. 96.

members. Deferring to the Clerk at critical junctures in the discussion of an issue, or relying on the Clerk to complete a minute after the close of the meeting rather than working through the minute within the meeting are two more common forms of deference. The danger here is that the meeting lacks full participation by the members. Expressed in Quaker terms the meeting needs to function, and functions best, when each member holds to their own "sense of the Light" in reaching decisions.

Reaching Unity

The unity that Quakers seek is a creative solution to often vexing concerns. Usually these concerns come before the meeting after prior discussions in meeting committees. However, some concerns may arise spontaneously during the business meeting itself. Barry Morley describes one such instance, which came about in his home meeting:

> At the end of business meeting the clerk asked if there was any other business. A woman Friend, Linda, stood up to say that she recently walked down the lane to the meeting house... but she broke off her story to cry. Friends waited. She then, a little more composed, resumed her story. It had been Memorial Day, and she saw men with guns in the Quaker graveyard. Another Friend tried to explain:
>
> 'There are men buried in the graveyard, who served in the military. The men were honoring them.'
>
> 'But they were in my graveyard with guns', Linda said through tears.
>
> Other Friends expressed sympathy with her distress. Others expressed anger that such a thing should be allowed. But once again the situation was explained:
>
> 'They're from veterans' groups. They decorate the graves of the veterans every Memorial Day.'
>
> 'After all', someone added, 'we knew they had served in the military when we allowed them to be buried there'.
>
> This looked like a stalemate. Then a Friend said:

> *'If a choice has to be made between Linda feeling as she does, and men with guns in the graveyard, that is not a difficult choice'.*
>
> *Linda's feelings. and those of others too, had now been taken note of and recognized. An older Friend asked Linda:*
>
> *'Do you have strong feelings about the veterans being remembered?'*
>
> *Having been heard, and hearing others, Linda was able to reply:*
>
> *'No. I have no objection to the men being remembered.'*
>
> *'Might we allow them to decorate the graves but leave their guns outside?'*
>
> *Suggested the older Friend. Another Friend supported this.*
>
> *'I can approve of that if it is acceptable to Linda'.*
>
> *'Yes,' said Linda, 'I would find that acceptable'.*
>
> *The meeting felt silent, and then adjourned.*
>
> *A year later, quite unexpectedly, Linda reported to the meeting that she had visited the graveyard on Memorial Day to check on the veterans.*
>
> *'They left their guns outside when they went in', she said.*
>
> *'The silence that followed', comments Morley, 'amplified the sense of unity we had felt a year earlier'.*[10]

This example shows what is essential to the Quaker practice. Quakers know that they have the right decision when they have unity. They know that they have overcome polarization and conflict. They create an opening, an implicit space, in which new understandings can emerge. The ability of a meeting to create this space rests in some measure on the skill of the Clerk to recognize the sense of the meeting, *and* the unity that it brings. He or she may discover this sense of the meeting by *trying out a minute* to

---

[10] Barry Morley, *Beyond Consensus,* p. 19f. Also quoted by Rex Ambler *TQW*, pp. 76-77.

see what objections or reservations may exist. Equally important, testing the minute in this way is a means to *find the form of the words* that best expresses the understanding of the sense of the meeting. When the final minute is written and accepted by the meeting, it is not just a record of the meeting's decision, it is a record of how the meeting came together to act on an issue.

Resolving issues in this way leads to great confidence in meeting decisions and a commitment by the members to follow through and carry out the decisions. By continually testing the practice meetings reinforce their understanding of how the practice works, and that they can place their faith in the practice. Witness Morley's comments (above) where the meeting's decision on the graveyard was tested a year later and "amplified the sense of unity we had felt a year earlier".

Some Finer Points

Attaining unity on an issue is not easy, especially in larger meetings. Gray areas can come about where the meeting is close to a sense of unity on a minute, but one or two members may have reservations about the minute. When these reservations do not rise to a point where the member objects to the minute the clerk may then ask the Friend whether he or she is willing "to step aside". Stepping aside preserves the unity of the meeting where the member with a reservation values the meeting's sense of unity over his or her reservation. The Clerk then records the minute in unity.

In modern meetings finer points of Quaker practice, like "stepping aside" in seeking unity, are often swept aside by members carrying over their experiences of making decisions in the secular world. Secular practices like caucusing, forming cliques, and politicking an issue before business meeting can easily swamp seeking unity. As meetings lose experienced members and experienced clerks the "not of this world" path is now more easily lost to the marketplace. As Barry Morley points out, the notion of "consensus" has slowly crept into Quaker speech when describing a meeting's decision process.[11] The pace of "sense of the meeting" is lost as meetings strive and succumb to a need to "make a decision" as they move through their agenda. In their desire to make a decision it is now more likely by consensus rather than by "sense of the meeting".

---

[11] Barry Morley, pp. 22-23.

6. A MINUTE IS AN EXPLICATION

Let's begin by looking at how we symbolize meaning. Gendlin's philosophy reverses the way we think about meaning.

What we call meaning arises from interaction between our experiencing and symbols.[1] When we attend inwardly to some aspect of our feeling, or our feeling sense of a situation, we use symbols (words and gestures) to make *that* feeling explicit. To initially hold a feeling in our attention, we use words like "this", "that" or "it" as markers to point to our feeling.[2] These markers have no meaning except to refer to our feeling. Once we symbolize (mark off) a feeling in this way, we can then further differentiate that feeling.

Gendlin makes the point that any aspect of our feeling can be symbolized and interpreted further. As he is fond of saying, "There is always more".[3] From a process point of view, we experience meaning when our symbolizing (and conceptualizing) carries our implying forward. Each explicit symbolizing can carry our on-going implying forward. Moreover at any place in our symbolizing we can pause and feel and let our words open into a wider implicit intricacy.

By understanding that there is always "more" to our implying than we symbolize and conceptualize, we can see that this way of symbolizing reverses how we commonly think about meaning. We commonly think that we create meaning when we speak and create order when we conceptualize. However, we experience meaning as a feeling or feeling sense. Our feeling sense of meaning is pre-conceptual. Our feeling sense arises in the

---

[1] Eugene Gendlin, *ECM*, p. 1.
[2] See the How Felt Meaning Functions in *ECM*, III pp. 90-137.
[3] *ECM*, p. 16.

body and is more "intricate" than any order that we symbolize.[4] We feel meaning as we sense into our on-going implying. Our feeling falls out of that sensing into our implying. We make *that* feeling explicit by speaking and thinking.

Further, when we say (or write) our felt sense of meaning we find that our words imply their own change. Our wording works by carrying our life forward in a situation. In expressing our sense of meaning each word or phrase that we use is its own occurring into the implying, its own carrying forward of its implicit sequences in a situation. When we speak or write we *use* this aspect of words, their own implying and carrying forward to carry us forward. In Gendlin's terms, we carry ourselves forward *mediately* (by means of) using words to express our felt sense of meaning in a situation.[5]

Explication

Now let us introduce a new implicit term, *explication*. Explication is what we do with the "more" in our feeling sense of meaning.[6] Explication is not only the "more", but a *new* whole implying. Our carrying forward makes a *new implying* from which we can speak. Implying (eveving) freshly makes its relevance in our seeking meaning. When we explicate we further differentiate our feeling sense of meaning "of" or "about" a topic or situation. Each word or word sequence that we put together is an occurring into our implying in the situation. We carry ourselves forward with each explicit sequence into our "seeking" to understand (and provide an understanding of) the situation at hand. More precisely, our implying in carrying forward is a whole new implying that leads us to say more. Our sense of order and structure arise from this, our living process.

From this implicit viewpoint, we can readily see that when a Quaker meeting reaches a decision and writes a minute, the process of deciding and writing a minute is a *group explication*. Within the meeting circle each member may speak from and about his or her feeling sense of their situation; each expression carries that member forward and may carry other members forward. Each member thinks and speaks from the "more" of his

---

[4] *ECM*, p. 24.
[5] *APM,* pp. 172-184.
[6] *APM*, pp. 143-145.

or her feeling sense of the situation at hand. The progression of expressions may carry the whole group forward, and the group may reach unity where there is an "Ah Ha!" moment where all feel a felt shift as the series of expressions fulfill a meaning "fit" to the situation, and the policy or problem before the meeting is solved. As the meeting carries forward with an explication, the explication changes what the situation "was". The meeting can live forward in ways which were not possible before.

Finding a Minute

Rex Ambler in his book on *The Quaker Way* tells of searching for a solution to a divisive problem that arose in his own home meeting of Birmingham:

> ... We had just received advice from Friends House (our central body) on how to comply with the Government's new law on child protection. Anyone who is given responsibility for children in any organization must have a police check on their past record to see if they have ever been guilty of abusing children. But it raised some of our hackles when it was presented to us in meeting. One male Friend wanted nothing to do with this interfering legislation, which implied that we trust no one in our organization, and suspect everyone as a possible child molester. Another Friend was very nervous about the implication that we might have such a molester in our midst, and was all in favour of implementing a tough policy. I didn't like the idea, because it seemed like we were being told what to do in our own meeting, over-riding any discernment that we might have. Shouldn't we perhaps resist the State on this occasion by refusing to comply with the law? It was a heated discussion, as you can imagine, and we were not going to get a uniting minute on this occasion. We called a Special Meeting. This time we sat in a circle without the [clerk's] table, and asked every one in turn – there were 10 or 12 of us –what we felt about the issue and what background was in our experience that led us to feel that way. The male Friend told us of his experience as a social worker, when he was deeply hurt by a false accusation (in court, I think it was) that blamed him for the mishandling of some children. The accusa-

> tion was withdrawn, but he didn't want to have to go through such an event again, or have it dragged up in the meeting. The woman Friend admitted that she felt very nervous with children anyway and was terrified of being asked to look after them herself. Her nervousness made her feel that 'looking after children' was a dangerous and dodgy business, so she was glad to have a test run on everybody. I said I didn't like being told what to do on this matter, and, on reflection – I surprised myself saying this – I didn't like being told what to do on any matter! When we had finally gone round the circle there was a sigh of relief. We knew now where we all were coming from. We saw no reason to disagree. Instead we found a policy that would feel right to all of us. We asked the Nomination Committee to find names for a 'children's committee' from a list of Friends who said they would be happy to work with children and happy to go through a police check for that purpose. We had a minute to that effect, and it resolved the issue on our minds.[7]

If we look at the sequence that Ambler describes, we see that the meeting was stuck in "a heated discussion" in their initial approach to coming up with a policy solution. The meeting members only began to gain a sense of expression when they gathered in a second meeting and began to say how they "*felt about the issue*" and "what background was in [their] experience that led [them] to feel that way". Speaking in this way let each member sense the "more" in his or her feeling response to the situation. A single round of expressions was enough to bring "a sigh of relief". This was a simple "Ah Ha!" moment, a felt shift in understanding the meaning of their situation out of the "more" of the many meanings open to them. The meeting found unity in solving their problem with a policy that "would feel right for all of us". They had found a "sense of the meeting".

Ambler does not provide a copy of the minute, but I can imagine it was simple as well. It could be something like: *The Meeting is united in asking the Nominating Committee to find names for Friends who are happy to work with children and are happy to go through a police check for that purpose...*

---

[7] Rex Ambler, *TQW*, pp. 70-71

In a closing comment, Ambler says that the issue did not rise again. "We knew that we had dealt with it properly".[8]

An explication rests at the heart of the Quaker business meeting practice of coming to a decision and writing a minute. Like many simple processes it is not easy to do. It is not easy to facilitate a group explication that achieves a felt shift in understanding and a unified "sense of the meeting". As we have discussed, facilitating an agenda with various issues and concerns relies on the experience and skill of the meeting Clerk (and the Elders) to guide the discernment, sense the trend in an issue, pick up on the bits and pieces of phrases that might help form a minute, and if necessary move the process forward with a trial minute. At the same time, the Clerk has to draw out the silent members to make sure she or he has an overall sense of the meeting. Often when the meeting comes to an understanding and achieves unity, the felt sense and felt shift can come swiftly – as in a sense of "Oh! That's it." "So, that's what we need to do." This was the case in Ambler's Meeting (above) dealing with their child protection issue. In my own experience clerking a meeting, I found that our meeting often achieved unity in an "Ah! Ha!" moment and a minute easily fell out of our discernment. Of course, there are always surprises. For example, I recall that our meeting took three business meetings to decide on the color of paint to paint the outside trim on the windows of our newly refurbished meetinghouse. At least we didn't rush to a decision. Rather we thoroughly seasoned it.

Next

Next we shall turn to look at another form of the gathering circle created by New York Quakers in the 1970's to work with prison inmates in seeking alternatives to violence.

---

[8] I am partial to this situation because my own home meeting faced a similar problem in the early 2000's when the state required getting a police check on adults working with children. We reached a policy similar to Ambler's meeting, but we had the advantage of having an experienced First Day School Committee in place that could look after implementing the policy.

7. AVP IS ANOTHER GATHERING CIRCLE

A *gathering circle* is the environment that Quakers have created with their silent meeting. So far we have used the term *gathering circle* interchangeably with Quaker meeting. However, that changed for Quakers in upstate New York in 1975 when inmates from the Green Haven Prison, a maximum-security prison, asked some visiting Quakers for help in putting together a program to reduce violence in the prison, particularly violence among youthful offenders.[1] In 1975 all of the major prisons in New York were still on edge following the lethal riots at Attica Prison in 1971 and were seeking ways to reduce violence in the prisons

The New York Yearly Meeting responded by working with the Green Haven inmates to put together a prison workshop program, which they called the *Alternatives to Violence Project (AVP)*.[2] In putting together AVP the meeting had to resolve several fundamental questions. Based on the changes the meeting made, we can imagine their questions: How much of the Quaker meeting practice could they carry over to a prison setting? This was a non-religious setting. What were they to say or do about the "Light within"? Time with the inmates would be limited. How would they establish the trust and deep listening that are fundamental to Quaker practice? Who would be willing to take on the task of putting together and facilitating the project? These questions were answered over time as AVP evolved in prison settings.

---

[1] Newton Garver and Eric Reitan, *Nonviolence and Community: Reflections on the Alternatives to Violence Project,* Pendle Hill Publications, 1995, p.3.
[2] AVP/USA, *Alternatives to Violence Project Basic Course Manual,* AVP Distribution Service, St. Paul, MN, 2002. Abbreviated as *AVP/USA.*

The Evolved AVP Program

As we shall see, the AVP program evolved by making the gathering circle more *explicit* and more *active*. Conditions like trust and learning about one another that develop over time in a Quaker meeting have to be developed *explicitly* (and *quickly*) in an AVP workshop. AVP facilitators lead a series of experiential exercises designed to develop trust, affirmation, listening skills, and problem solving skills. By using exercises and related activities like role playing the gathering circle becomes an *active circle*. The movement out of the circle into smaller groups and back again also makes the workshop *physically more active*. In AVP the gathering circle focus returns to the early Quaker's focus on personal change and transformation among the inmate participants.

While Quakers originally started and looked after the workshop program, after the first few years the New York Yearly Meeting "released" AVP from Quaker oversight. AVP became (and now is) an all-volunteer, community-based program offering workshops in prisons. AVP has grown into a national and international non-profit organization with local prison programs in some thirty-four states and two-dozen countries. In 2017 AVP conducted 1,090 workshops in 123 prisons in the US, training 15,687 inmate participants; 766 outside volunteers and 1,783 trained inmate facilitators facilitated these workshops.

The AVP Workshop

Each AVP workshop is an intensive (17-21 hours) workshop, which is usually held over three days. During these last 40 years AVP has developed workshops through the contributions of numerous facilitators. This collective wisdom is captured in the AVP workshop manuals. AVP manuals stress that AVP is concerned with process rather than content. Like the Quakers, in AVP the workshop experience is central. It is the *how* not the *what*. AVP manuals provide self-assessment and group exercises as well as brief co-operative games. This design creates an environment of community and trust that allows participants to seek and experience alternatives to violence. An essential ingredient to this process is that participation is voluntary, both for workshop participants and facilitators. AVP facilitators take part in the workshop's activities and exercises so that everyone present is both teacher and learner. Matters shared in AVP workshops are confidential.

Three Workshop Levels

AVP offers three workshop levels in a planned progressive sequence. The Basic (Level I) Workshop focuses on respect for oneself and others, communication skills, building trust, co-operation and community. It leads participants to practice specific conflict resolution skills through role plays. The second workshop, the Advanced (Level II) Workshop, provides an opportunity to go deeper into issues of conflict by following a theme. Typical themes include: communication, anger, relationships, power, or forgiveness. AVP sponsors further personal development by offering the T4F (Training for Facilitators) Workshop. Here participants experience a deeper level of learning by being part of a facilitating team, learning to manage and model the complexities of the AVP workshop process. On average it takes apprenticing in five workshops before a new facilitator becomes confident and competent in working with and leading the AVP workshop process. After facilitating five workshops AVP certifies the apprentice as an AVP facilitator. The same facilitator training is used for outside volunteers and inmate apprentice facilitators. AVP's use of inmate facilitators sets it apart from other prison programs. Once AVP starts to use a mixed team of outside and inside facilitators there is a enormous change in effectiveness in reaching and facilitating changes in inmates' attitudes and behaviors. When an inmate facilitator relates how he or she handled a conflict situation or describes a life-style change, it carries far more weight with inmate participants in the workshop.

Looking at the Basic AVP Workshop

I want to highlight the changes that AVP makes in modifying the gathering circle by looking in detail at some key elements in the AVP Basic Workshop. A Basic Workshop sequence of exercises and activities is: Icebreaking -> Affirmation -> Communication -> Intro to Transforming Power -> Cooperation -> Conflict resolution -> Role playing -> Reflection -> Wind-up.[3] In this progression each set of exercises and activities builds on what has gone before.

A workshop begins with inmate participants gathering in a circle with an AVP team of facilitators. All the participants including the facilitators

---

[3] This is the Manual's suggested sequence. AVP teams may vary the sequence.

are volunteers.[4] The facilitators then give a brief opening talk explaining how AVP works, going over some housekeeping rules and reaching an agreement with the participants on a contract for participating in the workshop, including an agreement to keep the personal sharing in the workshop confidential.[5]

Marking Off the Workshop – The Adjective Name Game

Once the opening talk is done a facilitator immediately leads the group in the Adjective Name Game. Here is the Manual's description:

> *Say your first name and a positive word that describes yourself and begins with the same letter or sound as your name. Example: "Gorgeous George." Repeat the names of all those who went before you, then give your own. Continue around the circle until you get back to the first person, who then has to do the whole group.*[6]

The Name Game sets out several key markers in the AVP workshop. First, it starts an affirmation process for the inmate. Inmates rarely view themselves in a positive way. The Name Game is a start in this process. Second, it immediately lets inmates get to know one another. Participants are asked to give their workshop names when they talk, or to use another's workshop name when addressing another participant. And third, the Name Game sets the workshop apart from other prison activities. Almost all inmates have "yard names". These are nicknames that they acquire and use in the prison. Using AVP names effectively marks off the AVP workshop experience as something completely different for the participants. At the end of this initial activity most inmates have a sense that AVP is going to be different than anything that they have experienced before – in or out of prison.

---

[4] AVP suggests limiting a workshop to twenty participants. The facilitator team may vary from two to six with four as an average number.
[5] *AVP/USA*, pp. A-11-A-12.
[6] *AVP/USA*, p.F-18. My own AVP name is Harmonious Harbert.

A First Exercise in Affirmation and Communication–Concentric Circles[7]

One of the elements in Quaker meetings is the deep listening that functions in the gathering circle. In AVP this type of listening is made explicit by using listening exercises. Many AVP programs start their program with a listening exercise called Concentric Circles. Here the facilitator divides the groups in two by having the participants count off by one's and two's. The one's are asked to form a circle with their chairs facing outward, and the two's are asked to form a circle with their chairs facing inward towards the one's. This creates a circle of pairs with the participants in each pair facing one another. The facilitator tells the participants that she (or he) will provide them with a topic that they will talk about for **two minutes**. While the first person talks, the second in the pair will listen without talking. Their roles will then be reversed. The second will talk and the first listen. When they are done, they are to thank each other, and those in the outer circle are to move one chair to the right. The process is repeated with a new topic. Here are some sample topics:

Someone that I admire and why.
Something good that happened to me on the way to growing up.
A part of me or my life I want to work on this next year.
Some ways other people can help me grow toward my goals.

As a facilitator you notice that the first few rounds of talking/listening are hesitant, but usually after the third round the energy level and focus pick up. By the end of the exercise, a few inmates are usually reluctant to give it up. For many this is the first time that they have had someone listen intently to what they have to say about a topic close to them.

After ending the facilitator asks the group to reform in a larger circle. She or he then leads the group through *processing* the exercise by asking the participants to share what they experienced.

Action with Light & Livelies[8] – Big Wind Blows

While the facilitators have some fifty-plus Light & Livelies to choose

---

[7] *AVP/USA*, pp. E-19-E-20.
[8] These are cooperative games for children that Quaker meetings have collected over time. Of course, they are not called "children's games". The name "Light & Livelies" works well.

for their agenda, a common first choice is the Big Wind Blows because it is simple, easy and active. Here is the Manual's description:

> *There are just enough seats in the circle for everyone but you. You are the Big Wind, and whomever you blow on has to move. Instead of blowing, you call out, 'The Big Wind blows on everyone who ...' and then add your own description; for example, 'on everyone who wears black socks,' or, 'everyone who has two ears.' Everyone who fits the description must get up and exchange seats; in the general commotion, you try to get a seat also. Whoever is left standing there, gets to be the Big Wind next time. If the Big Wind calls 'Hurricane' then everyone has to change seats.*[9]

The Big Wind gets the participants up and out of their seats. There always are a few creative types, for example calling out glasses, sock and bandana colors to narrow the Big Wind blowing on one or two selected participants. The game easily peaks when you get one or two Hurricanes in a row. The effect of this game and other Light & Livelies is to relieve tensions that arise from exercises. It also helps create a sense of community and energizes the workshop group.

Gathering Circle

A three-day AVP workshop will have eight or nine sessions, each lasting 2 or 2 ½ hours. Depending on how the agenda develops, each session usually starts with a gathering circle. Since the first workshop session starts with an introductory talk, the first gathering circle usually starts the second workshop session.

Quakers will recognize an AVP gathering circle as carrying over a lesser-known form of the Quaker meeting called "worship sharing". This is a responsive gathering, which Quakers use in a variety of ways. It is used when Quakers meet to "thresh out" an issue. Members respond to a question on an issue by going around the circle and sharing their responses. It is sometimes used by the Meeting Clerk in Business Meeting to elicit responses from the members on a pressing issue. It also is used in the sharing that follows a Light meditation.

---

[9] *AVP/USA*, F-8.

AVP uses the gatherings to build a sense of community. Community is created by each participant gaining some sense of the humanity of other participants in the group. After forming a circle, the facilitator leading the gathering will then set out the topic and give a response from her own experience. Then, she will pass on the turn to give a response to the person to her right (or left). Each participant takes his or her turn moving a response to the topic around the circle. Most participants willingly respond. It is rare for participants to consistently pass in a gathering. Facilitators use the gathering to set a tone, go deeper, or lighten a mood for a session. Here are some sample statements for a first gathering session:[10]

To be a good listener, I must...

I get along well with others best, when...

An important lesson that I have learned is...

For many inmate participants the first day of an AVP workshop is challenging and can be the start of a life-changing experience. As the participant's responses move around the circle in a gathering as a facilitator you can sense some responses resonating and interaffecting inmates as their own experiences are picked up and expressed again in new ways. Later in small groups they will have more chances to interact at this human level. In this type of gathering the AVP team also gains some insight into how individuals are faring, and also gains a *sense of the group*.

A Gathered Workshop

As the workshop moves on the gatherings can explore deeper issues. In those gatherings the participants can reach a deep level of trust and sharing, especially when the topic touches the raw parts of their lives. One such gathering occurred when the topic was "How violence has affected my life ..." In that instance one participant described how he had stabbed and killed his own brother. His story so moved the gathering that the facilitator called for minutes of a covering silence as the inmates shared in his sorrow and the hope for forgiveness emerging out of his and their own damaged lives.[11] In this instance and in others, the gathering is covered in

---

[10] *AVP/USA* pp. F-2-F-5.
[11] This instance is unusual in that it is uncommon for an inmate to talk about his or her crimes. Personal Communication from Joyce Victor.

the same way a meeting is covered when the speaking on a theme moves the whole group to a climax with a felt sense of sharing in their own living.

Transforming Power – An Organizing Experience

Usually on the second day, AVP introduces the idea of Transforming Power. As you may recall we talked about what the Quakers might do, or not do, with their reliance on the "Light within" in organizing an AVP workshop. Transforming Power replaces the Quaker's Light within" as an organizing experience in AVP. Transforming Power is the experience of power that comes to us when a felt sense forms and we transform a conflict situation into a peaceful outcome.

The use of Transforming Power in AVP comes from a booklet by Larry Aspey called *Transforming Power for Peace*.[12] Larry Aspey was a member of the New York Meeting's Peace and Social Action Committee, an AVP founding member and a key early facilitator. Under his leadership using Transforming Power became a central organizing idea in AVP workshops. In addition, several of the early Quaker facilitators had participated in the civil rights movement in the 1960's. Many had participated in non-violent direct actions and marches, and had helped train participants in non-violence with role playing exercises in southern churches and other organizing settings for non-violent direct action. For the Quakers, this group provided experience with facilitating non-violence, and equally as important provided support for *Transforming Power* based on their own transforming experiences in non-violent direct actions.

One or more facilitators will introduce Transforming Power in a talk about their own experience in transforming a potentially violent situation into a positive outcome. Most commonly, the facilitator visually introduces Transforming Power in the form of a mandala.[13] "Transforming Power" is in the center. There is an inner ring with the phrases "respect for self" and "caring for others"; and an outer ring with the phrases, "think before reacting", "expect the best" and "ask for a non-violent solution".[14]

---

[12] Quoted from Newton Garver and Erics Reitan, *Nonviolence and Community*, pp. 11-12.

[13] Stephen Angell introduced the mandala in an AVP newsletter: "The AVP Mandala", *Transformer*, Summer 1994.

[14] *AVP/USA*. p. B-54. This is the simplest form. There are more elaborate forms of the mandala.

How Do You Know When You Have Transforming Power?

The key to understanding Transforming Power (TP) is to experience what it feels like. The Manual (and most TP talks) set out what it feels like:[15]

You experience it as an AHA!!! moment.

You experience a spirit of caring.

You feel as if you are letting go of something.

You feel right about what you say or do.

And you lose your fear if you had any.

Following this introduction, most AVP teams then lead an exercise in sharing stories of Transforming Power. Almost all inmate participants can recall and recount a situation where they were able to resolve a potential conflict non-violently.

Pausing and Letting

If you look closely at what AVP describes, you will see that we are on familiar ground. Transforming Power is another way of describing the forming of a felt sense. It is what I call an *active form*. Rather than "holding and letting", I prefer to use the phrase "pausing and letting", pausing the present conflict situation to let a felt sense form, then experiencing a felt shift as the situation is carried forward. In conflict situations, unlike meditation and focusing, the pausing and letting can happen quickly and a person can experience a felt shift with an amplified sense of power. *Ah! You have the power within you to change and transform this violent situation into an alternative peaceful outcome.* This is the organizing idea for AVP workshops.

Among the mandala phrases, "think before you react" is critical and it is the phrase that sticks with the inmate participants, particularly when they actively engage in using their AVP skills in seeking alternatives in situations that confront them. In order to let a felt sense form you need to pause and hold the situation – expressed here as "think before". Once the participants get (and experience) this pausing, then they are able to respond as alternatives to violence can and do form for them. And they begin to gain confidence in (what we are saying) is their sense of implying in the situations that they face.

---

[15] *AVP/USA.*, B-11.

Communication Skills[16]

After an introduction and exercises with TP. AVP sets out a series of exercises to develop communication skills that are helpful in pausing a conflict situation. AVP puts forward a series of dialogue exercises called "I Messages".[17]

However, when facilitating dialogue exercises in a Basic AVP, I prefer using exercises based on Marshall Rosenberg's Nonviolent Communication (NVC).[18] I think NVC provides a better understanding of how feelings and needs function in a potential conflict situation. I also like NVC's emphasis on coming up with a *doable request* based on expressed needs. In NVC we have yet another way of describing a felt sense forming. When a felt sense forms, NVC refers to what comes to carry the situation forward as a "need". Rather than the Quakers "truth", NVC describes the felt sense forming as responding to our human need to carry our living forward. The following is an NVC exercise on experiencing feelings and needs.

An NVC Empathy Exercise on Feelings and Needs

An AVP facilitator starts this exercise by brainstorming about human needs.[19] She can quickly generate a list with needs like meaning, self-worth, acceptance, consideration, love, respect, trust, play, and nurturance (food and water).

On a second sheet divided with a line down the middle she brainstorms a list of feelings. On one side she writes feelings when our needs our met, and on the other when our needs are not met. The facilitator takes a need, say acceptance and asks, "How do you feel when you are accepted?" She gets response of feelings like "contentment", "thankful" … And when she asks, "How do you feel when you are not accepted?" She gets "annoyed", "angry", "resentful"… She quickly gets two lists and the understanding

---

[16] Please see Harbert Rice, *Language Process Notes*, Focusing Institute, 2008, pp. 75-95 for a more extended discussion of NVC-based dialogue.

[17] *AVP/USA*, pp. E-29-E-35. The "I Messages" are based on Tom Gordon's work with children.

[18] Marshall Rosenberg, *Nonviolent Communication,* Puddle Dancer Press, 2002.

[19] Brainstorming is just asking participants to quickly call out a human need and writing the list down on a newsprint sheet. For a list of needs, see Marshall Rosenberg, pp. 54-55.

that feelings point to and are part of our needs in any given situation. We carry forward when our needs our met, and we are stuck when our needs are not met. Further, Marshall Rosenberg makes the point:

All violence arises from unmet human needs.

Having generated lists of needs and feelings, the facilitator can start the empathy exercise. I like this exercise because it leads to a clear understanding that feelings and needs are bodily felt and bodily sensed. The facilitator starts by saying that she is going to do an exercise to look to see what feelings and needs we have when we recall a situation where our need was met, and a situation where our need was unmet.[20]

Two facilitators model the exercise while the participants look on. They will work with the two situations, recalling when a need was met, and when a need was unmet. One facilitator recalls her situation, the second facilitator acts as a listener and coach. They then may switch roles.

The active facilitator starts by recalling a situation where her need was met. She briefly describes the situation that she is going to use. (The fewer words the better to avoid any narrative.) The second facilitator provides empathy by listening and reflecting as the active person reports on her feelings. If necessary, the second person can coach by gently asking, "What are you feeling?" "Can you point to where you are feeling?" The active facilitator points to her body.[21] Then, she moves to sense what her needs were. "What are you needing?" She again points to where in her body that she senses her needs. Both feelings and needs may shift until the person comes to "rest" after finding and expressing one need. When she comes to "rest" a palpable shift occurs. You can see a felt shift occur as the body eases, color comes to the face, and breathing deepens and slows as relief comes. Some NVC facilitators call this extended moment "resting in the beauty of the need". If you are coaching a participant who is experiencing

---

[20] When doing the exercise it is important to ask the participants to select situations that they are willing to share with the group. This tends to minimize the risk of a participant re-traumatizing herself (or himself) when recalling a situation where a need was not met.

[21] As in Focusing, feelings and needs are most often sensed in the thoracic area of the body.

a felt shift resting in a need, you will feel your own body respond in an empathetic way. If you have been tense, you too will feel your tenseness ease.

After modeling the process, the facilitators do the exercise by pairing the participants. Each participant takes a turn at working with each situation.[22] The responses that you see are revelatory, revelatory in the sense that many participants are working with feelings and needs that were ignored, unknown, or long suppressed. When working with a situation where a need was unmet, many inmates find relief in just recognizing what their need was and resting in that need. "Oh, that's what I was needing!"

Looking at this exercise from an implicit point of view, we can readily see that this is an exercise in "pausing and letting", letting a felt sense form. We can understand that:

> *Feelings and needs are aspects of interacting with our implying to let a felt sense form in an NVC dialogue process.*

In a conflict dialogue we intend to pause the situation in symbol space to let a solution form in implicit space. We bodily sense and say our feelings and needs. Our relevant need is a way forward in the situation. Our formed felt sense also will include *a felt sense of the other person and his or her needs*. Our sense of the other person's needs is quite vague. NVC recognizes this vagueness and encourages guessing in a dialogue. "I'm guessing that you are disappointed. And that you need some reassurance from me". "Can you say what you are needing?" Needs are not pre-determined possibilities. We only know the relevant need after we meet the situation and carry forward. A felt sense further solidifies as we find the "need" that fits.[23]

Expressed in AVP terms, when a felt sense comes to a person in a conflict dialogue that is an Ah Ha! Transforming Power (TP) moment. When an expressed need and an empathetic response occur with a formed felt sense both antagonists are carried forward. A doable request that comes may be quite simple. "Would you be willing to meet later to talk this thing

---

[22] If the facilitators believe that the participants may struggle with expressing their needs, they may provide the participants with a list of needs from Marshall Rosenberg's book.

[23] A felt sense only needs to form for one person in a conflict situation. If it forms with a felt shift, the other person will "know" that a solution is at hand with an empathetic resonance and a shift in his or her own implying in the situation.

through?" How the situation may work out may be vague at first, but both can sense that a solution is at hand and that they "can work it out".

The NVC Dialogue Process

After the feelings/needs exercise the team often moves on to an exercise that leads the AVP participants through practicing a four-step dialogue process, either with scenarios of their own choice or selected scenarios. They write out and share their four-step dialogues. Here is NVC's four-step dialogue model:

Make an observation about the situation you are in.

Say how you feel.

Identify and say your need.

Make a request based on your need.

Here are some key points about the NVC dialogue process.

First, any dialogue will not move forward without empathy and self-empathy. By empathy we mean simply a willingness to be with the other person in the situation; and by self-empathy we mean a willingness to be with your self in the situation. Dialogue requires both empathy and self-empathy. If empathy is not present, the conflict situation (the pattern of words and actions) will assert itself.

Second, we need to pause the situation to sense our feelings and needs.[24] Pausing ("think before") is the most difficult element in dialogue. An AVP team sometimes explores what it takes to pause by using an Advanced AVP exercise called "Triggers" as a follow on exercise to the dialogue exercise. In the Triggers exercise the team divides the group into smaller groups of three, and asks the participants to identify and discuss those words and actions that trigger a violent response. "Your mother is a ......" Many find common triggers. More importantly identifying and knowing your own triggers helps in pausing a situation. It is an early warning signal that we can use to help to break a response pattern. When we are in a conflict dialogue we are actively in the symbolizing pattern (words and actions), which we are trying to change. We need to pause the pattern

---

[24] Pausing is a different activity. See *APM*, pp. 206-215.

of words and actions in order to let a felt sense of our need form. We need to pause the conflict pattern while we are in the pattern.

And third, NVC emphasizes making *doable requests*. We make a request to meet our need in the situation, "Would you be willing to…?" We are seeking common ground to meet our need and the other person's need as well. Affirming the other person and having our own expressions of need affirmed means you have reached common ground with some level of trust. When a felt sense of a solution forms we still need to make doable requests. This is the "working out" of the situation to carry forward. NVC emphasizes that dialogue is not linear; it often is recursive. In facilitating the dialogue exercise the facilitator says, "Don't be surprised if your first request receives a 'No'". "Expect to do another round and more of feelings and needs to create another request". As we make these requests a felt sense can form and re-form in the situation. If a solution does not form, we can expect to experience pain and suffering. Revealing our feelings and needs makes us vulnerable. Still, any experience of change, especially change in a conflict situation, is revelatory as we realize that change itself is possible, even under dire circumstances.

Role Plays[25]

After learning about Transforming Power (TP) and working to acquire some dialogue skills, AVP's next focus is on role plays. Role plays are short scenarios of potential conflict situations, where the participants may find alternative non-violent solutions. AVP's role plays are adapted from role play techniques developed during the civil rights movement in the south in the 1960's. There are several forms, but in the most common form AVP facilitators divide the group into three or four teams. A facilitator works with each team to develop a one-act scenario. The key to creating a scenario is that it has the potential for violent conflict, but that the outcome is open-ended. The outcome is not fixed and the dialogue is not fixed. When teams make up their scenarios more often than not they choose a common situation: an outside situation like "road rage", or a "family conflict" where a daughter comes home late without explaining where she has been; an inside situation might be "cutting in the mess hall line", or a "commissary deal gone bad".

---

[25] *AVP/USA*, pp. G-2-G-12.

Each team assigns characters, say two protagonists with supporting characters for each protagonist. Each team develops a backstory to set the scene and one team member tells the backstory, setting the scene and introducing the characters. Each team plays out its scenario before the larger group acting as the audience. The team's facilitator acts as a director and starts the play by calling "action"; and signals the end by calling "cut". The plays may become intense, and facilitators have to follow the action closely, for example calling "cut" if it becomes too emotional or an inmate moves to lay a hand on another participant. Alternatively, if the scenario moves to a conclusion where Transforming Power is found in an alternative solution, or if a path to an alternative becomes clear, then the facilitator's call to "cut" is easy. However, many scenarios present an impasse where there is no solution and the action dwindles. Here the director calls a "cut" to move on. After a call to "cut", the facilitators move to *debrief* the characters, learn about their experiences in the role play and help them return to the larger group.

Despite the fact that a role play usually lasts just five or six minutes, there is a wealth of experience and information that the play may yield. The facilitators use the debriefing to draw out the players' experiences. All the facilitators share in the debriefing with each facilitator debriefing a player. The facilitators start with the person who was most emotionally involved in the play:[26]

> *Let's find out what happened.*
>
> *How do you feel right now?*
>
> *What was running though your mind when... What did you notice/think?*
>
> *What was the turning point for you? How did it relate to TP (Transforming Power)?*
>
> *Are you satisfied with what happened?*
>
> *Are you ready to get out of character and return to the group?*
>
> *Who are you now? Please say your AVP name.*

---

[26] *AVP/USA* p. G-5.

> *Is there anything that you would like to say to your character before you return to the group?*

Debriefing may take half an hour or more, even in cases where the players reached an impasse. After debriefing when the larger group discusses the role play, participants may comment on alternatives that may have been present during the play, but were not played out. Finally, tensions often arise during the plays and many inmates use their roles and certainly their debriefs to inject some humor into the activity – offering some memorable one-liners as they tell their less-than-stellar character to get his or her act together.

The Workshop's Ending

At the end of the workshop the AVP facilitators close the workshop with a series of activities: answering any unanswered questions that arose in the workshop, announcing further workshops, asking for written evaluations from the participants about the workshop and handing out workshop certificates. In a few prison systems the inmates receive credit hours for the AVP workshop. In most prisons the inmates keep their certificates in their own personal files, but ask to have a copy put in their permanent prison file. Inmates often use the certificate and talk about their experience in AVP during their parole hearings.

Closing

The final activity in the workshop is a closing. The amount of time left often dictates the type of closing. If time is tight the team may elect to do a "Tennessee Squeeze". This is a simple closing circle where the group stands, locks arms and moves the circle in and out.[27] If more time is left, the team may elect to do a different closing such as "Gift Giving". Here a facilitator starts off the giving by turning to the person on his or her right and offers a gift (from the workshop) that he thinks might help the participant. The gift may be general: "I give you the gift of patience", or it may be specific: "I give you the gift of patience to work through your family situation". The gift giving then moves around the circle and ends with all locking arms one last time.

---

[27] *AVP/USA*, pp. F-20-F-23.

A Gathered Closing

I have already answered a natural question: "Do AVP workshops experience a gathered workshop in the way that Quakers experience a gathered meeting?" In my own experience, the answer is a simple "Yes". As we have seen, a covered gathering can occur during any part of the workshop, but most often during one of the later deeper gatherings in the workshop.

However, it also can occur at the end of a workshop during the workshop's closing. Rather than a single theme drawn out in a Quaker meeting (or in a single workshop gathering), a closing gathering comes from the cumulative effect of all the changes and transformations that have occurred in, among, and between the participants in the workshop. In that final tight workshop circle there is an uplifting sense of joy. Many facilitators and participants cry and linger talking, wiping away tears, unwilling to make the break away from the workshop until time forces their departure.

The Facilitator's Role[28]

An AVP facilitator performs a similar role in the workshop to that of the clerk of the meeting in Quaker meeting. Facilitating requires many of the same skills, especially the skill in "reading" participants in the workshop, and "reading the sense of the group". Reading the sense of the group also includes sensing the energy of the group. At times, especially in the afternoon, a group's energy may sink. A facilitator then may call for a Light & Lively or a more active exercise to raise the energy level back up. Facilitating in AVP differs from Quaker's clerking because it is a team effort. AVP discourages any attempt at solo leadership.

As in Quaker meeting, the skills of the team can and do influence the outcome of the AVP workshop process. In a mature AVP program the team usually includes a lead facilitator, an experienced facilitator and two apprentices at different stages in their training.[29] The lead facilitator acts as liaison with the prison administration, which means getting clearance for outside persons coming in, scheduling all the logistics for the workshop, place, times, notifications for inmates, etc. He or she is the contact person interacting with prison personnel during the course of the workshop.

---

[28] *AVP/USA*, pp. C-2-C-16.
[29] Again, when a team is training more facilitators the team may have six (or rarely more) facilitators.

Preparation

Substantial planning goes into preparing for a workshop. If the prison administration allows a planning meeting on a day (or evening) prior to the workshop, then an AVP team can meet with all outside and inside facilitators to plan the workshop. A planning meeting begins like all AVP meetings with a short gathering. In this planning meeting the team selects the facilitators who will do the workshop. There are usually more inmate facilitators than outside facilitators, so slots for inmate facilitators are at a premium. After some discussion the team selects the facilitators for the workshop team, balancing experience with bringing along apprentices. Many AVP teams follow the Quaker practice of making their decisions with the "sense of the group".

Once the team is selected, the next step is to put together the three-day agenda. The lead facilitator usually provides a draft agenda. The team looks it over and suggests modifications. Here having inmate facilitators is invaluable. They usually have a better "feel" for what exercises and Light & Livelies will work with a prospective participant group. Each workshop team member volunteers for roles in leading the various exercises, Light & Livelies, agenda introductions and evaluations in each session. The apprentices have first choice in selecting their roles. Finally, the planning meeting ends with a closing and well wishes for the workshop team.

Clinicing[30]

At the start of the workshop the team members get together briefly to go over the agenda, confirm their roles, and set up the workshop, preparing agenda sheets, posting the community agreements, etc. During the gatherings and when the group is in the larger circle, the team members space themselves around the circle. This practice provides them with a better view of the participants to get a "read" on how individuals are responding to the workshop. A common problem encountered early on in workshop, for example, is having inmates who are intimate try to pair up (sitting side by side) in the circle, or trying to volunteer for the same group when the larger group breaks up for an exercise. The facilitators may decide to intervene to minimize the pairing.

---

[30] Some AVP teams use the term caucusing.

During the workshop getting the team together to discuss a problem or to adjust the agenda is called *clinicing*. Any team member can call for a *clinic*. While the AVP Manual provides time estimates for each item in the agenda, exercises often run long or the team may have to adjust the agenda to a change where security, for example, is late releasing inmates for the workshop. If it is not in a break, the team actually *clinics* in a team huddle in the center of the larger circle. The lead facilitator simply tells the group the team is going to clinic to adjust the schedule. The decision to adjust is made by a "sense of the team".

Of course, teams clinic when more serious problems arise, as when an exercise goes awry and the team has to regroup and recover some flow in the workshop. Or, the team may sense that the group is drifting in an afternoon session and they need to add some energy with a Light & Lively or a short exercise that requires some movement.

Gangs are prevalent at every security level in the prison. AVP takes all volunteer inmate participants, and in some prisons the lead facilitator may specifically ask to include inmates from varied ethnic and race background and ages. Most AVP workshops will have members from different gangs in a workshop. Their presence simply requires another level of awareness for the team, "reading" how these members are responding to the workshop. The inmate facilitators are more attuned to the dynamics of participant interactions and may provide a "heads-up" if any altercation is in the offing. In practice having various gang members present is more likely to break the other way. In AVP they can and do come to see one another in a human way. I know of at least one instance where opposing gang members reconciled and settled their differences in a workshop.

End of Day and End of Workshop Reviews

After the end of a workshop day the team meets to assess how the workshop went. The assessment includes getting a combined "read" on each participant and a "sense of the group" as a whole. The group reviews the ups and downs of the exercises Light & Livelies, gatherings and closings, what went well and what will need some work. This review includes feedback from each team member in assessing how one another did, comments include both positive feedback and "constructive criticism", especially for the apprentice facilitators. AVP has a hundred or more exercises. Learning to facilitate the exercises is a daunting process.

The team does a final end of the workshop review on the last day. This review is the same as an end of the day review, but the team also has the written evaluations of the participants, which are given out and completed before closing the workshop. These evaluations aid in the assessments of both the individuals and the group as a whole. Recall that when the facilitators are not leading an exercise or a Light & Lively, they are participating in the workshop activity. In their self-assessments of their own participation, they often undergo and report changes in their life outlook and relationships. At the end of a workshop almost all facilitators report feeling both exhilarated and exhausted.

Next

Next we shall look at the changes and transformations that AVP inmate participants experience and report.

8. CHANGE AND TRANSFORMATION

Since the gathering circle in AVP uses explicit exercises and activities, we have far more information about the changes and transformations that occur in AVP workshops as compared with Quaker meetings. Also, unlike Quaker meetings, AVP teams document their workshops with written notes and reports. We have three main sources of information about the AVP workshops: (1) direct feedback from inmate participants in the written evaluations that they fill out at the end of a workshop; (2) observations from AVP facilitators in their notes and reports on workshops; and (3) a few objective studies looking at specific outcomes for inmates, like looking at the recidivism (return) rates of released inmates who have taken AVP workshops.

The following sections on Changes and Transformations are taken from a report on AVP in New Mexico Prisons.[1] Since 2005 the AVP team in Northern New Mexico (AVP-NNM) has given AVP workshops in New Mexico prisons. AVP-NNM provides workshops in both men's and women's prisons. AVP does workshops in one men's prison (PNM) in Santa Fe, NM. It provides workshops in two women's prisons. One prison is in Grants, NM, and another facility is in Springer, NM. There are about 6,640 men incarcerated in the NM system, and about 760 women. The men's PNM is a maximum-security facility with some 790 inmates. The women's facility in Grants has about 370 inmates, and Springer, which is a lower security facility, has more than 400 inmates. Springer is severely overcrowded. The rated capacity at Springer is 268 inmates. The AVP-NNM team has trained inmate facilitators in all three prison facilities.

1. Inmate Feedback

In the New Mexico prison system the first effect that we see with AVP is the rate at which inmates choose to advance to the next AVP level. On

---

[1] Harbert Rice, Margaret Willen, and J.J. Tellatin, *Alternatives to Violence in New Mexico Prisons*, Report of Alternatives to Violence Project of Northern New Mexico (AVP-NNM), 2017. Report is available on request.

average about 60% of the inmates who have taken a Basic workshop go on to take an Advanced workshop, and of those, again about 60% got on to take a facilitator training (T4F) workshop.

AVP-NNM like many AVP programs asks each inmate participant to make a written evaluation in the workshop's final session. AVP-NNM has collected 12 years of these evaluations from the women's prisons. Rather than cherry pick from 12 years of written comments, the AVP-NNM report simply takes the comments from a Basic workshop as a sample of the type of response seen in the evaluations.[2] The following comments are condensed to avoid repetition.

> *How the workshop changed how I will deal with violence in the future ...*
>
> *I will stop and think before I act.*
>
> *I am more aware of how I can easily mishandle a situation so that I can react differently.*
>
> *Taught me new techniques to use.*
>
> *It made me more aware of the different solutions that can be used instead of violence.*
>
> *I will take time out to think before reacting and not hang around the same people or people that want to make me mad.*
>
> *My most significant personal learning during the workshop was ...*
>
> *To know that I have come a long way and to keep going.*
>
> *How to listen to other people and try to understand why someone feels the way they do.*
>
> *I could be myself and enjoy all the exercises and activities without being negative.*
>
> *What I learned about myself, and having to use positive affirmation often changed my views on different situations.*
>
> *There's not always a time that I must turn to violence. I can use positive words to solve my problems.*

---

[2] *Alternatives to Violence in New Mexico Prisons*, p. 5-6. These responses are from a Basic workshop held in the women's facility in Grants, NM in December 2016.

Dealing with past feelings that have been bottled up. It helped me forgive and forget in a positive way.

I learned a lot about myself, my thoughts and feeling towards violence, and need for peaceful solutions.

What I would say to someone considering taking the workshop is ...

It is excellent and a great learning experience.

That it is worth the time and effort to have a healthier way to be.

Just try it – it might work for you. It helped me.

This class will change how you think about your life.

I would let them know it's a very good, informative, and fun workshop that will have you thinking/acting different.

It is worth the hours because they make a difference in the way you think.

If you really participate and pay attention, it will help make you a better person.

It's fun and you learn the person you are and can become without violence.

2. Observations

Besides these types of written participant comments, AVP facilitators are able to observe attitude and behavioral changes in inmates as they progress through a workshop, and as they progress through the three workshop levels.[3] We see positive changes in self-esteem and self-motivation; communication and relating to people; choice and responsibility; and problem solving. Critically, we see the participants acquiring attitude skills in self-awareness, empathy, and personal responsibility.

Self-Esteem and Self-Motivation

The first and most noticeable effect we see in an AVP workshop is an increased sense of self-esteem and self-awareness. The first exercise in the Basic workshop starts a process of affirmation and self-respect that continues throughout the AVP workshops. The

---

[3] I have drawn on many of these observations in discussing how the AVP Basic workshop functions.

changes our team observes are changes in self-perception where the participants see their own self-worth as a human separate from their own bad choices and actions. More often than not, this change in perception is expressed as a form of knowing "that I am not a bad person", and "that I have made some bad choices". From the Basic we also see an increased motivation to change, expressed as a sense of direction or a next step, of "a need to grow".

Communication and Relating to People

AVP facilitates developing communication skills, particularly listening skills. We are able to observe changes in participants as they develop these skills. These changes are part of a complex process. We can, however, see three clusters of changes: (1) developing trust; (2) seeing other's viewpoints; and (3) gaining an understanding of feelings and actions.

Trust is the most difficult issue faced by inmate participants in changing how they communicate. AVP workshops generate a sufficient sense of community and safety so that the participants can, in their words "open up", and talk about themselves. We can observe this change directly by the energy level and intensity of conversations in the workshop, but more importantly by changes in perception of what it means to risk trusting – "like me, people need a chance to be trusted."

With opening up and trusting comes the ability to understand another person's viewpoint. We often hear comments like "I can open up and listen to what other people have to say". Or, in the written comment above: "How to listen to other people and try to understand why someone feels the way they do." Participants learn that empathy can deter violence.

With a shift to talking about their own and other's feelings, we see a qualitative change in how the participants are communicating. This change is essential in dealing with the more difficult issues of remorse and forgiveness that each inmate faces. We hear comments like "I'm better able to define and identify my feelings"; and comments on understanding "how our feelings cause our actions".

Choice and Responsibility

With the ability and confidence to communicate more effectively, we see changes in how workshop participants approach situational conflicts. The first change that we observe is an understanding that each situation provides choices and consequences arising from those choices. Inmates report that they are better able to "stay open minded in a conflict"; "come at it from another angle, seeing the other side"; and realize that "the consequences of my actions today" will lead to "my tomorrow". Understanding that each situation provides for choices goes hand in hand with an understanding that "we all must accept responsibility for our actions".

In the Advanced (Level II) Workshop, the inmate participants select the workshop theme. Their clear first and second choices have been workshops on Forgiveness and Relationships. In both of these workshops, we observe inmates focusing on taking responsibility for past decisions and actions as they seek to repair or resolve family issues and other relationships. The inmates clearly understand that working through conflicted relationships is a critical and essential step for a successful re-entry back into a community.

Problem Solving

Realizing that there are choices and consequences to our actions leads to seeking alternatives when faced with difficult issues and situations. In a sense, this is the end outcome sought in AVP. As we have discussed, AVP encompasses the idea of seeking alternatives with the phrase "think before reacting". You see this in the first written comment above: "I will stop and think before I act." When inmates describe how they have dealt with a difficult situation, we often hear them refer to this AVP phrase, usually in a form indicating that they have integrated it into their own thinking.

To stop violence in any conflict situation, particularly in an escalating situation, a person must pause or hold the situation in order to create alternatives. This understanding and the ability to act on this understanding are absolutely critical to finding alternative solutions in real-life conflict situations. Pausing and holding a situation before acting is the main AVP intervention point in changing existing patterns and cycles of violence. The type of feedback that we receive from workshop participants shows quite clearly that they understand this point. The participants often tell us they are eager to share this and other AVP tools with their families so that the next generation benefits as they seek to break cycles of violence.

What's More

Finally, you may have noticed that the last written inmate comment above, talking about AVP said, "It's fun ..." Prison counselors and correctional officers (CO's) are often surprised and bewildered when they hear periodic laughter coming from an AVP workshop. The laughter often comes from the short active co-operative games, the Light & Livelies. Besides providing an emotional outlet, the games provide another form of co-operation and community building. Inmate participants uniformly describe the workshops as "fun". Strange as it may seem at first: AVP workshops are both life changing and fun.

3. Studies in AVP Outcomes

The types of changes that the AVP-NNM team observes are consistent with those seen in other more established AVP programs where objective studies have documented long-term behavioral changes arising from AVP workshops.

Two important questions addressed in these studies are: Do changes experienced in AVP workshops persist? And, more importantly, do they carry over when an inmate is released?

The most-studied AVP program is in the Delaware prison system. The following two studies were done on an AVP program at the Delaware Correctional Center (DCC). DCC is a medium security men's prison with about 1,000 inmates. The AVP program at DCC was at least 10 years old at the time of the studies. The first study by Stanton Sloane (2002) looked at the effect of AVP on behavioral infractions ("write-ups") before and a year after taking AVP workshops. The second study by Marsha Miller and John Shuford (2005) reported on the effects of AVP on the one-, two-, and three-year cumulative recidivism rates in the DCC.

Write-Ups[4]

Stanton Sloane studied a group of 400 inmates before and after they took an AVP workshop. All the inmates were sentenced for violent crimes and most had multiple offenses. Most had sentences over 15 years. Sloane's study results showed a 60% drop in write-ups for the AVP group a year after completing an AVP workshop. As Sloane suggests in discussing his results, behavioral infractions (write-ups) are a good, robust measure of behavioral changes. Write-ups represent a broad spectrum of misbehavior ranging from relatively minor rule infractions, like possessing contraband, to violent interactions with other inmates or correctional officers.

If you look at the type of changes we see in New Mexico, particularly changes in self-awareness, attitude, and confidence in communicating with others, these are just the set of social skills that allow an inmate to successfully change his or her behavior across the range of situations that he or she encounters in the prison environment. In a series of interviews with inmates after the study, Sloane reported that inmates: had developed self-respect and respect for others; had developed communication skills; had expressed undertaking alternative approaches to conflict situations; and that AVP had established a reinforcing social community within the prison.

Recidivism[5]

Marsha Miller and John Shuford reported on the effects of AVP workshops on the recidivism rate at the DCC. Miller and Shuford studied the one-, two-, and three-year cumulative recidivism rates for 175 men who had taken AVP and had been released in the ten years prior to the study. They used inmates who had attended a volunteer Life Skills class as a control group. The three-year cumulative recidivism rate for the control group was 58.3% and the rate for the AVP group was 31.1%, showing a reduction of 47%.

---

[4] Stanton Sloane, *A study of the effectiveness of Alternatives to Violence workshops in a prison setting*, Unpublished master's thesis, 2002.

[5] Marsha Miller and John Shuford, *The Alternatives to Violence Project in Delaware: A three-year cumulative recidivism study*, 2005. Available from AVP/USA.

Further, since AVP attempts to effect changes in violent behavior, Miller and Shuford also studied the felony recidivism rate. They found that the cumulative three-year violent re-offending rate for AVP men was 5.7%, indicating that AVP not only lowered the recidivism rate, but that it substantially lowered the violent re-offending rate. Most of the AVP men's re-offending offenses were non-violent.

As these two objective studies show, AVP workshop outcomes persist over time with changes in specific behaviors.

What Sets AVP Apart from Other Prison Programs

AVP's view is that the changes and transformations that we observe result from changes in the inmate participants' attitudes. AVP's experiential workshop process can and does change attitudes. Attitudes come from life experiences. If attitudes are to change, the change must come through a life experience. In the AVP workshop training, the facilitators help the participants create a community or container based on a culture of trust, respect and caring. This container of safety is a transforming element in the workshop. In the same way that a Quaker meeting can lead to a gathered meeting, the gathering circle in the AVP workshop provides a safe place where the inmates can let down their barriers and defenses. In effect, they "let down their masks" and experience life at a more basic human level. This is a powerful experience. It is a cultural shock. The experience can and does lead the participants to a commitment to change.

Next

Let's turn next to look at how AVP has developed from an implicit point of view.

9. AVP IS AN ADAPTIVE PROCESS

As you have seen, the Alternatives to Violence Project (AVP) workshops look quite different than a Quaker silent meeting for worship. Still, the gathering circle is at the heart of each group gathering. How then are we to consider the changes made in and for AVP from Quaker's practice?

AVP Is an Adaptive Process

Please recall that the present Quaker worship meeting and the attendant monthly meeting came about when the early Quakers were confronted with the stoppage in the life of the Society that came from the fall of James Nayler. The environment, the gathering circle that the Quakers created in response to Nayler, has remained fairly constant since that time. However, the gathering circle in AVP that the Quakers created with help from Green Haven inmates did not come from a stoppage. Rather it came from a desire to adapt Quaker practices, particularly the Quaker commitment to nonviolence, to serve a radically different population, a prison population. This prison population is secular, segregated (by gender), and further segregated by the level of security risk that different inmate groups pose.

The Quaker response (to the inmates' request for help) is what I term an *adaptive process*.[1] The Quaker response has been to make a series of changes to the gathering circle to adapt it to work in prisons. These adaptations came about through the efforts of many early facilitators. No one leader, like the early George Fox, emerged to lead this process. Rather, the changes were incremental responses in early workshops. Again, we can assume these responses arose from facilitators, or teams of facilitators "holding and letting", holding the "life of the workshop" in their workshop evaluations and discussions, and letting change come from their implying in those situations. AVP's adaptive responses come from that aspect of our

---

[1] The adaptive process that arises with occurring into implying is neither predetermined nor random. Rather it is a more intricate ordering coming from our implying. See *APM* 4A, pp.38-50, and *APM* 5A, pp.79-80.

implying that we experience as responsive to our needs, as a *responsive order*. Further, we see that this ordering process is socially adaptive. Our occurring into implying is a socially adaptive process.

We discussed some of these changes made to the gathering circle when we introduced AVP. There were three main changes: making the circle more *explicit*, making the circle more *active*, and making the circle more *structured* by introducing a progression of activities in the Basic workshop. Each of these changes responded to a "need" to carry the workshop forward.

Making the workshop *explicit* responded to the need to bring out hidden elements of the Quaker meeting, like affirmation, communication, and cooperation. Making the workshop circle *active* responded to the need to encourage participation in the workshop, and with the Light & Livelies make the workshop physically active so that participants were not sitting for long periods of time.

As we have said, the AVP gathering circle with the passing of a topic around the circle is a copy of the less well-known Quaker practice of worship sharing. This type of gathering is a *responsive* gathering. Quakers use this gathering when a special meeting is called to "thresh out" a meeting concern. They use a responsive gathering to start the threshing meeting, or use it during the meeting. In AVP the gathering circle is a constant throughout the workshop. If you visualize the workshop as a Scottish Country Dance, the gathering circle is formed, dissolved and reformed throughout the workshop day. It is the beginning and the end. It is where inmates express themselves, revealing what they are experiencing and what they hope to change in their lives.

Finally, the *structure* of the Basic workshop responded to a need to aid inmate participants in finding points in their experiencing to change their attitudes and behaviors. Recall the basic sequence is: Ice-breaking -> Affirmation -> Communication -> Intro to Transforming Power -> Cooperation -> Conflict resolution -> Role playing -> Reflection -> Windup. In this progression each set of exercises and activities builds on what has gone before. Providing this structure responded to a need to focus on the change and transformation of and for the individual participants. The workshop still creates a sense of community. The sense of community contributes to and helps foster the trust that the workshop creates for the inmates. In medium and maximum-security prisons where the sentences are longer and include many "lifers", a sense of community exists among the inmate facilitators. If you ask an inmate facilitator with a long sentence why he (or she) is doing AVP, a common answer is that they are doing it as a "community service".

Transforming Power

In discussing Transforming Power, I suggested it is both an experience and an idea. I emphasized experiencing transforming power because I wanted to point out that it is an aspect of a formed felt sense when we carry forward in a situation, especially a conflict situation. However Transforming Power is also an organizing idea. It is one of the few elements that AVP facilitators teach in an AVP workshop. When introducing Transforming Power (TP) in a workshop, some facilitators say that since TP is available to all, it is a wider power that we share and can tap into. This adds a mystical aspect in suggesting a wider power in Transforming Power for the inmates to relate to.

As Newton Garver and Eric Reitan comment, "Transforming Power is an awkward phrase".[2] Despite being awkward and sounding like jargon, its advantage is that it comes without historical baggage. Early AVP facilitators wanted to avoid words like "God" and "love" because they considered that inmates could associate these words with repression, denial and even abuse. On the other hand the word "Power" possesses an attraction for inmates since it suggests making choices and getting control of their life situations, which is what AVP wants its participants to try to do. Further, TP incorporates the phrase "think before you react". Again, this is precisely the intervention point that AVP teaches to break cycles of violence.

AVP is now forty plus years old. The workshops are stable in the sense that the overall form is not changing. There are continual improvements as facilitators exchange new exercises and new Light & Livelies. Old exercises that perform poorly are dropped or modified. Still, Transforming Power has proved its worth as an organizing experience and idea. It has fulfilled the AVP founders' need to replace the Quakers "Light within" and "truth" as a core experience.

---

[2] Newton Garver and Eric Reitan, pp. 11-14.

Some Limitations of AVP

Some AVP teams also give AVP community workshops. These workshops may be done with specific groups, like gangs or new immigrant groups. More often community workshops are used as a means to recruit people to become facilitators and to go into prisons to facilitate AVP workshops. These community workshops usually use some version of the AVP Basic Workshop. In my own experience the results from these workshops are mixed. Some individuals are deeply moved and go on to become AVP facilitators. However, many participants are unmoved and not touched in any meaningful way by the workshop. These community workshops rarely show the group cohesion that develops in prison workshops. This simply may reflect the fact that community participants are not in anything like the "dire straits" of prison participants. We on the outside lead comfortable lives and can easily step aside from any challenge that an AVP workshop might present. The net result is that AVP is primarily a prison program in the US and most countries.[3]

Adapted Gathering Circle

In summary we can say, the Quakers have created (with the help of inmate facilitators) a gathering circle for AVP that nourishes change and transformation in the lives of its prison inmate participants. Like the silent meeting the workshop's gathering circle creates a sense of community. On occasion the gathering circle can and does lead to a gathered workshop where the participants experience an unbounded joy as the whole group carries forward. AVP's gathering circle is now fully adapted to work in prisons and is no longer tied to the Quakers. Having been "released" from Quaker oversight, AVP now has a "life of its own" as it works in US prisons, and other prisons abroad.

---

[3] AVP has been used in other situations. For example, AVP was used as a reconciliation program following the Rawandan massacres in 1994.

10. THE FUTURE OF QUAKER PRACTICE

EPILOGUE

Any discussion of the future of Quaker practice must begin with a look at the number of Quakers.[1] In 2016 there were an estimated 76,000 Quakers in the US. In colonial times one-third of the population was Quaker. Quakers have been in decline for several hundred years. The same is true in the UK. The UK Quaker numbers are estimated at 16,000. Most Quakers are now pastoral (programmed) Quakers. There are more pastoral Quakers in Guatemala (20,000) than silent meeting members in the UK. The largest Quaker population is 146,000 in Kenya.[2]

Certainly these numbers in the US put us in the position of a field biologist trying to decide if a highly endangered species will survive. Since Quaker meetings keep members on their meeting rolls until a member requests to be taken off or dies, the numbers of practicing Quakers in silent meetings in the US and the UK are likely lower than the aggregate numbers suggest.

Part of the decline in numbers is inherent in Quaker practice itself. Quaker practice is a small group practice. Recall that Quakers want and need to see each other when they gather. Quakers grew only by replicating the monthly meeting, but have not yet solved the question of scale. Even a yearly meeting can test the current limits of Quaker practice.

---

[1] These numbers are from: http://quakerspeak.com/how-many-quakers-are-there-in-world/
The US numbers also include members of the Quaker Church, a pastoral form of Quakers.

[2] Kenyan Quakers also are an evangelical form of Quakers with pastors and hymns. They like to say that they are "noisy" Quakers.

The iGen Generation

While the current Quaker numbers are bleak, Quaker prospects seem even bleaker if we look at our newest generation, the iGen generation.[3]

The iGen generation is the first generation that has grown up with a smart phone. They were born between 1995 and 2012.[4] (The iPhone came out in 2007.) In the US, they number some 74 million, about 25% of the population. They are now in high school and college.

They are in no hurry to grow up. They go out less, date less, and have less sex than previous generations. They learn to drive later and are less likely to have a job while in high school. They are less religious and less spiritual both publicly and privately than previous generations. More to the point, they spend almost all of their leisure time, an average six hours a day, on their iPhone and the Internet, texting and following social media.[5]

The net effect is that they choose to interact more online rather than in person. Here is Kevin (age 17) describing his generation.

> *I feel like we don't party as much. People stay in more often. My generation lost interest in socializing in person – they don't have physical get-togethers, they just text together, and they just stay at home.*[6]

Interacting via text and social media means that this generation lacks social skills. They simply do not spend the time interacting in person that will enable them to relate and communicate with others, either their peers or adults. Here is Athena (age 13) speaking to this point:

> *We grew up with iPhones, we don't know how to communicate like normal people, and look people in the eye and talk to them.*[7]

This sketch is an overly broad view of iGen teens. They are more tolerant of other's views, more work focused and more realistic about their

---

[3] Jean Twenge, *iGen*, Atria Books, 2017.
[4] *iGen.*, pp. 5-6.
[5] *iGen.*, pp. 18-47.
[6] *iGen*, p. 69.
[7] *iGen*, pp. 90-91.

future prospects in study, work and family life. However, for Quakers these teens and young adults simply represent a newer, more encompassing cultural trend running over and against the Quaker practice of sitting in silent meeting where in-person communications play a key part. It is hard to say if this cultural trend will persist. Many iGen teens recognize that they are addicted to their phones, but like any addiction it is hard to break or lessen the habit. Since most modern Quakers come to participate in meeting via convincement, individuals from this iGen generation may simply come to convincement later in their lives than previous generations,

Decline in Numbers

Let us look more closely at the decline in Quaker meetings. I believe the decline in numbers, which Quakers are experiencing and have long experienced, comes from several factors. The Quakers share in the recent declines in church membership in the US. However, the Quakers decline started long before the decline in church membership in the US and UK. The decline began with the evangelical mass movement in the 1700s, continued in the 1800s with pastoral schisms, and continued further in the 1900s with the ascent of liberal Quakerism where social actions were encouraged, but religious differences were often left unresolved.

I think the decline is due in large measure to three factors.

First, as Rex Ambler points out, the Quakers did not, and have not set out a way to teach their early worship practices. Throughout the Quaker decline, new members and attenders were largely left on their own to assimilate Quaker practice in silent meeting. So long as communities and families were stable, this practice could sustain meetings as their numbers declined. However, modern cultural mobility works over and against the time required to assimilate Quaker practices without some form of formal (or informal) introduction to sitting and speaking in meeting.

Second, the decline in meetings experiencing the climax of a gathered meeting has led to a hollowing out of the meeting for worship. This hollowing out is linked to the lessening of the spiritual depth experienced in meetings. I think the lost depth comes in part from ambivalence among many modern Quakers about the Biblical Christianity expressed by early Quakers. In effect, modern Quakers are cut off from the inspirational source that carried early Quakers forward. Now, with yet more diverse religious views in meetings, religious differences persist in modern meetings that are unable to gather.

And third, the words Quakers use to describe and explain their own experiencing, "Light" and "Truth", no longer attract or compel people to follow a Quaker way. While the practice itself is not easy, words that are fading and have lost resonance with large numbers of people make it yet more difficult to attract newcomers to participate in and support meetings. Still, as we have seen in AVP the gathering circle can live on in an adapted form independent of Quakers.

Recognizing the decline in meetings and the difficulties in gathering a meeting with diverse religious views is not new. In a practical way these issues come into focus among those Quakers in yearly meetings tasked with revising the Advices and Queries when they issue of new *Faith & Practice*. How are they to describe Quaker faith in and for the modern meeting? Such is the case in the UK where a task group (RPG) recently formed to explore expressions of Quaker faith.[8] While the group took up the task of exploring expressions of the split between theism and nontheism, they soon moved beyond these labels to explore the challenge of "finding ways to communicate the depths and significance" of worship in silent meeting.[9]

One among many insights that arose within the task group was an understanding that how Quakers use and understand the use of language sways how Quakers express their faith. In particular, Quaker language is a Christian language. It reflects a Christian story. While modern Quakers may use multiple names for the divine, they still refer to the experience of the "Light within" and the need for "testimony".[10] Without an understanding of how we create meaning modern Quakers may lose the life carried forward in these expressions.

It is well beyond my leading to say how Quakers should communicate their faith arising from their experience in meeting. However, what I can do is point to the key intersect where Gendlin's insight of the Implicit and Quaker practice cross. This key crossing is how we create meaning and carry life forward when a felt sense forms for us in meeting. All past ex-

---

[8] Helen Rowlands (Ed.), God, words and us. Quaker Books, 2017.
[9] Helen Rowlands, p. 2.
[10] Helen Rowlands, pp. 53-54.

periences, including a Christ-consciousness are embedded in our Quaker language. Failing to understand that we can experience and carry forward the life embedded in our common Quaker language cuts Quakers off from their roots.

At this point, let's just say that the Quaker practice of sitting in silent meeting as we know it is likely to continue to decline in the US and the UK. However, so long as Friends meet there is always the possibility that they may reignite their meetings, or in Thomas Kelly's phrase they may "rekindle the embers" of their meetings.

What Have We Gained?

What have we gained then by looking at Quaker practice by crossing Gendlin's Implicit and the Quaker's "Light within"?

I think we have gained an understanding of Quaker practice as creating an environment, which we have called a *gathering circle*, where change and transformation for both individuals and the group can occur. As we have shown from an implicit point of view, working and living within and for the circle is a social process. The Quaker's silent meeting shows that "holding" a situation and "letting" a felt sense form is central to the practice. Both individuals and the meeting as a whole can experience a felt shift as they are carried forward. The Quaker's *gathered meeting* is that rare and coveted time when the whole of the meeting group carries forward.

Quakers created the current form of the meeting (and the monthly business meeting) from a stoppage following the fall of James Nayler. When New York Quakers created AVP as an adaptation of the silent meeting circle for work in prisons, their AVP work shows that the gathering circle environment is not limited to Quakers and Quaker practices. Rather, the adapted gathering circle can and has flourished in helping thousands of prison inmates transform their lives. Like its meeting counterpart, the AVP gathering circle in prison can lead to a *gathered workshop* where the whole workshop group carries forward. The AVP workshops now live on independent of the Quakers.

As we point out, we can talk and think about the Quaker practice as an underlying implicit social process. We can talk about Quaker experiences in process model terms. The evolving form of the Quaker "Light meditation", Rex Ambler's resurrection of George Fox's early writings is Ambler's meditation crossed with Gene Gendlin's Focusing.[11] In this meditation, the expression of *light symbolizes implying,* and the expression of *truth symbolizes what carries our living forward.* In the same way, the Quaker's term of "leading" is the working out of the implicit sequences that arise with a formed felt sense. In seeking to describe the Quaker's meeting for business, we find that we can extend the meaning of Gendlin's term of "explication" to understand the "writing of a minute" as a *group explication process,* the unfolding of the *more* in the group's implying of a situation.

Looking at Quaker practice from an implicit point of view does not take away from the experiences of countless Quakers in sitting in silent meeting. However, thinking from the implicit let's us see Quaker practices in a different way, different in the sense that we are viewing the Quaker process from a different point of view, crossed with but now different from the terms Quakers use to describe their own practice. We can talk about and think about a gathering circle without depending solely on Quaker terms. Further, we look at what we have gained in understanding about how the Implicit functions in a group setting. Here we are indebted to the long history of the Quakers in writing about their meetings for worship, their monthly meetings for business and their social testimonies.

An Arc of Awareness.

Inherent in Gendlin's work on the Implicit is an evolution of our human awareness of our own living process. If we look at Gendlin's successive environments (spaces), we see that behavioral space is embedded in symbol space (the environment that we create with our use of language), and symbol space is embedded in implicit space, the environment that we create when we interact with our implying. Traversing this succession of spaces leads us to ever more intricate patterns of living *and* ever more awareness of our own living process. As Gendlin suggests, letting a felt sense form in implicit space is a natural process. The difference for us now is that we *knowingly* seek to let a felt sense form, and seek to live, however fleetingly in implicit space. In effect, we return again to Quaker roots – as "seekers of the truth". Seekers now with a further modern understanding that the truth we seek is the change in our implying that will carry our living forward and help to carry our fellow seekers forward.

---

[11] Now carried forward through the *Experiment with Light Network.*

Mystery of the Implicit

There is one major difference between Quaker terms and the terms put forward here from the implicit process model. Quaker terms largely have remained fixed. Gendlin's terms, as he tirelessly pointed out, are open. They can be thought about further, and extended or changed. They are not fixed. At some point in time someone will extend or find better terms and concepts to describe our living process. We can expect then that we will gain a better understanding of the Quaker's gathering circle and the changes and transformations that it fosters and supports.

One process model term is not defined, our *implying*. We can understand *occurring* as we speak and act into and out of our implying, but in occurring into implying, implying holds out the "more" in our living. It is beyond our grasp. It is always "more". As we have said when we interact with our implying to let a felt sense form, how we choose to express our experience rests with our situation and our past experiences. If we come as Quakers, we may express our experience as waiting upon the "Light within", the "Light of God", or the "Divine". If we are engaged in Focusing, we may simply say that we were letting a "felt sense" form. However we choose to symbolize our experience, the heart of our experience remains a mystery. Our philosophical work here in looking at Quaker practices does not take the mystery out of sitting in silent meeting. If anything, it may even deepen the mystery. Our living at its core still remains a mystery.

REFERENCES

AVP/USA, *Alternatives to Violence Project Basic Course Manual*, AVP Distribution Service, St, Paul, MN, 2002. Abbreviated as *AVP/USA*.

Angell, Stephen, "The AVP Mandala," *Transformer* (AVP Newsletter), Summer 1994.

Ambler, Rex, *Light to live by*, Quaker Books, 2002. Abbreviated as *Ltlb*.

Ambler, Rex, *The Quaker Way*, Christian Alternative Books, 2013. Abbreviated as *TQW*.

Ambler, Rex, *Truth of the Heart*, Quaker Books, 2001. Abbreviated as *TotH*.

Apsey, Larwence, Bristol, James, and Eppler, Karen, *Transforming Power for Peace* (2nd Revised Edition) Friends General Conference, 1981.

Britain Yearly Meeting of the Religious Society of Friends, *Quaker Faith & Practice* (4th Edition), 1995-2008.

Friends General Conference, *The Wounded Meeting*, Friends General Conference, 1993.

Gates, Tom, *Worship "The Gathered Meeting Revisited*, Philadelphia Yearly Meeting, 2011.

Garver, Newton and Reitan, Eric, *Nonviolence and Community: Reflections on the Alternative to Violence Project*, Pendle Hill Publications, 1995.

Gendlin, Eugene, *A Process Model*, Northwestern University Press, 2018. Abbreviated as *APM*.

Gendlin, Eugene, *Experiencing and the Creation of Meaning*, Northwestern University Press, 1997. Abbreviated as *ECM*.

Gendlin, Eugene, *Focusing* (2nd Edition), Bantam Books, 1981.

Gendlin, Eugene, "Thinking Beyond Patterns" in *The Presence of Feeling in Thought*, B. den Ouden and M. Moen (Eds.). Peter Lang, New York, 1991.

Gendlin, Eugene and Hendricks, Mary, "Thinking at the Edge: A New Philosophical Practice" in the *Folio*, Vol.19, No. 1, 2004.

Kelly, Thomas, *The Gathered Meeting*, The Tract Associations of Friends, 1947.

Kelly, Thomas, *The Eternal Promise*, Friends United Press, 1977.

Lampen, John (Ed.), *Seeing, Hearing, Knowing*, Sessions, 2008.

Miller, M.L., and Shuford, J.A., *The Alternatives to Violence Project in Delaware: A three-year cumulative recidivism study*, 2005. Available from AVP/USA.

Morley, Barry, *Beyond Consensus: salvaging the sense of the meeting*, Pendle Hill Publications, 1993.

Rice, Harbert, *Language Process Notes*, The Focusing Institute, 2008.

Rice, Harbert, Willen, Margaret, and Tellatin, J.J., *Alternatives to Violence in New Mexico Prisons,* Report of Alternatives to Violence Project of Northern New Mexico (AVP-NNM), 2017. Report is available on request.

Rosenberg, Marshall, *Nonviolent Communication* (2nd Edition), Puddle Dancer Press, 2002.

Rowlands, Helen (Ed.) *God, words and us*. Quaker Books, 2017.

Sheeran, Michael, *Beyond Majority Rule* (2nd Edition), Philadelphia Yearly Meeting, 1996.

Sloane, S., *A study of the effectiveness of Alternatives to Violence workshops in a prison setting*, Unpublished master's thesis, 2002.

Steere, Douglas, *The Quaker Meeting for Business*, Southeastern Yearly Meeting, 1982.

Twenge, Jean M., *iGen*, Atria Books, 2017.

West, Jessamyn, *The Quaker Reader*, Pendle Hill Publications, 1962

ABOUT THE AUTHOR

Harbert Rice is a Quaker. His home meeting is the Reno Friends Meeting in Reno, NV. He served as Clerk of the Reno Meeting for several years. He is now retired and lives with his wife Rebecca Mueller on a small farm in Dixon, NM.

He trained as a research biologist and has a PhD in plant biology. He has done basic research on red light mediated plant developmental processes. However, at various time he also has been a seaman, a gardener, an environmental researcher, and a publisher of computer books. He has done volunteer service in hospice and was a founding team member of the Alternatives to Violence Project (AVP) of Nevada, which introduced and facilitated AVP workshops in the Nevada State Prison System.

He studied Eugene Gendlin's *A Process Model* with Rob Parker. He also served as a Member of the Board of Directors of the Focusing Institute. The International Focusing Institute is an international non-profit organization set up by Eugene Gendlin to promote the use of *Focusing* and to house his philosophical works.

This book, *A Quaker's View Of Gendlin's Philosophy* (2020) is Harbert's second book on the Philosophy of the Implicit. His first book is *Language Process Notes: How We Use Words To Get Beyond Words*. (2008).

Harbert can be reached at: www.embudovalleypress.com.